Skilled Trades Assessment Readiness Study Guide

Practice Questions, Detailed Explanations, and Math Refresher for the Canadian Trades

Test Preparation Inc.
WWW.TEST-PREPARATION.CA

Copyright © 2025 Complete Test Preparation Inc. All Rights Reserved.

Intellectual Property Rights This publication is protected by copyright. No part of this book may be reproduced, copied, distributed, or transmitted in any form or by any means—including graphic, electronic, or mechanical methods such as photocopying, recording, or information storage and retrieval systems—without the prior written permission of the publisher, except in the case of brief quotations embodied in critical reviews and certain other noncommercial uses permitted by copyright law.

Disclaimer & Limitation of Liability While the publisher and author have used their best efforts in preparing this book, they make no representations or warranties with respect to the accuracy or completeness of the contents. The advice and strategies contained herein may not be suitable for your situation. Test content and administration rules change frequently; readers are advised to verify all information with the official test providers. Complete Test Preparation Inc. shall not be liable for any loss of profit or any other commercial damages, including but not limited to special, incidental, consequential, or other damages.

Non-Affiliation Notice Complete Test Preparation Inc. is an independent publisher and is not affiliated with, endorsed by, or sponsored by any testing organization, educational institution, or government agency mentioned in this publication. All trademarks, service marks, and trade names are the property of their respective owners and are used for reference and identification purposes only.

Complete Test Preparation Inc. is not affiliated with the makers of the Skilled Trades Exam, who are not involved in the production of, and do not endorse this publication.

ISBN-13: 9781772455991

Version 10 December 2025

About Complete Test Preparation Inc.

Why Choose Complete Test Preparation? You want to spend your valuable study time where it counts the most. We've got you covered.

Since 2005, we have helped hundreds of thousands of students succeed with over 145 study guides and online courses. We know that tests change, which is why we keep our content current and relevant.

Study with a Purpose With this purchase, you are doing more than just preparing for a test. You are supporting a mission to improve education globally. We are proud to support charities that bring learning opportunities to those who need them most.

Learn more about our mission:
https://www.test-preparation.ca/charities-and-non-profits/

You have definitely come to the right place.
If you want to spend your valuable study time where it will help you the most - we've got you covered today and tomorrow.

Thank you for studying with us!

Feedback

We welcome your feedback. Email us at feedback@test-preparation.ca with your comments and suggestions. We carefully review all suggestions and often incorporate reader suggestions into upcoming versions. As a Print on Demand Publisher, we update our products frequently.

CONTENTS

6   **Site Prep & Setup - Getting Started**
        How this study guide is organized   7
        The Skilled Trades Test Study Plan   8
        Making a Study Schedule   11

14   **Interpreting Specs, Codes & Manuals**
        Reading Comprehension for Trades
        Answer Key & Solutions   22
        Help with Interpreting Written Material   23
        Drawing Inferences And Conclusions   30

34   **Toolbox Math - Basic Math for Trades**
        Answer Key & Solutions   42
        Basic Math Video Tutorials   46
        Fraction Tips, Tricks and Shortcuts   46
        Converting Decimals to Fractions   52
        Percent Tips, Tricks and Shortcuts   53
        Exponents: Tips, Shortcuts & Tricks   55
        Order Of Operation   61
        Classroom to Job Site:
        The "Shop Math" Translator
        How to Convert Word Problems   62
        Part 1: The Trade Math "Dictionary"   63
        Part 2: The "Wastage" Trap   64
        (and how to avoid it)
        Part 3: The Canadian Context
        (Metric vs. Imperial)   64

67   **Applied Trades Science**
        Self Assessment   68
        Answer Key & Solutions   76
        Basic Physics   78
        Energy: Work and Power   82
        Defining Force & Newton's Three Laws   85
        Force: Friction   88
        Fundamental Forces: Electromagnetism   89
        Fundamental Forces: Gravity   92
        Speed, Acceleration and Force Problems   94

98	**Understanding Mechanical Systems**	
	Answer Key & Solutions	109
	Overview of Simple Machines	112
117	**Spatial Visualization**	
	Self-Assessment	120
	Answer Key & Solutions	128
	Folding Tutorial	129
134	**The Dry Run**	
	100 Questions - Full Topic Coverage	134
	Answer Key & Solutions	180
195	**The Final Inspection**	
	100 Questions • Full Topic Coverage	
	Answer Key & Solutions	237
253	**The 3-Step Search** **Speed-Reading for Technical Manuals**	
	Summary Checklist: The Speed Reader's Mindset	256
257	**Digital Trades Data Entry, Graphs, and Tablet Testing**	
	Graph Literacy (Trends vs. Numbers)	259
	Data Entry & "Drop-Down" Discipline	261
	Tablet Navigation (The "Hidden" Menus)	262
	Summary Checklist: Digital Readiness	263
264	**Diagnostics & Troubleshooting**	
	What to do after you take a practice test	264
265	**Getting the Most from Practice Questions**	
267	**Job Complete**	
268	**Digital Toolbox**	

Site Prep & Setup

Welcome to the First Step of Your Future. You have set a goal to enter the skilled trades, and this test is the gateway. But you shouldn't just aim to take the test—you should aim to crush it.

Getting a high score opens doors. It proves to employers and unions that you have the discipline and the aptitude for the job. Yes, studying requires dedication, but if you focus your energy now, you will soon be holding that acceptance letter.

Where do you start? Right here. It is normal to feel unsure of how to prepare. That's where we come in. This guide maps out everything you need to know, boosting your competency and your confidence.

The Skilled Trades Entrance Test

The Skilled Trades Test has four sections, interpreting written Material, applied math (number sense, geometry, algebra), mechanical reasoning, and general problem-solving.

While we seek to make our guide as comprehensive as possible, note that like all exams, the Trade Entrance Exam might be adjusted at some future point. New material might be added, or content that is no longer relevant or applicable might be removed. It is always a good idea to give the materials you receive when you register to take the Skilled Trades Test a careful review.

How this study guide is organized

This study guide is divided into four sections. The first section, self-assessments, which will help you recognize your areas of strength and weaknesses. This will be a boon when it comes to managing your study time most efficiently; there is not much point of focusing on material you have already got firmly under control. Instead, taking the self-assessments will show you where that time could be much better spent. In this area you will begin with a few questions to evaluate quickly your understanding of material that is likely to appear on the Skilled Trades Test. If you do poorly in certain areas, simply work carefully through those sections in the tutorials and then try the self-assessment again.

The second section, tutorials, offers information in each of the content areas, as well as strategies to help you master that material. The tutorials are not intended to be a complete course, but cover general principles. If you find that you do not understand the tutorials, it is recommended that you seek out additional instruction.

Third, we offer two sets of practice test questions, similar to those on the Skilled Trades Test.

The Skilled Trades Test Study Plan

Now that you have made the decision to take the Skilled Trades Test, it is time to get started. Before you do another thing, you will need to figure out a plan of attack. The very best study tip is to start early! The longer the time period you devote to regular study practice, the more likely you will retain the material and access it quickly. If you thought that 1x20 is the same as 2x10, guess what? It really is not, when it comes to study time. Reviewing material for just an hour per day over the course of 20 days is far better than studying for two hours a day for only 10 days. The more often you revisit a particular piece of information, the better you will know it. Not only will your grasp and understanding be better, but your ability to reach into your brain and quickly and efficiently pull out the tidbit you need, will be greatly enhanced as well.

The great Chinese scholar and philosopher Confucius believed that true knowledge could be defined as knowing what you know and what you do not know. The first step in preparing for the Skilled Trades Test is to assess your strengths and weaknesses. You may already have an idea of what you know and what you do not know, but evaluating yourself using our Self-Assessment modules for each of the areas, will clarify the details.

Making a Study Schedule

To make your study time the most productive, you will need to develop a study plan. The purpose of the plan is to organize all the bits of pieces of information in such a way that you will not feel overwhelmed. Rome was not built in a day, and learning everything you will need to know to pass the Skilled Trades Test is going to take time, too. Arranging the material you need to learn into manageable chunks is the best way to go. Each study session should make you feel as though you have accomplished your goal, or at least are closer, and your goal is simply to learn what you planned to learn during that particular session. Try to organize the content in such a way that each study session builds on previous ones. That way, you will retain the information, be better able to access it, and review the previous bits and pieces at the same time.

Self-assessment

The Best Study Tip! The very best study tip is to start early! The longer you study regularly, the more you will retain and 'learn' the material. Studying for 1 hour per day for 20 days is far better than studying for 2 hours for 10 days.

What don't you know?

The first step is to assess your strengths and weaknesses. You may already have an idea of where your weaknesses are, or you can take our Self-assessment modules for each of the areas,

Exam Component	Rate 1 to 5
Interpreting Written Material	
Toolbox Math	
Fractions	
Decimals	
Percent	
Algebra	
Basic Science	
Chemistry	
Basic Physics	
Spatial visualization	
Mechanical Comprehension	

Making a Study Schedule

The key to making a study plan is to divide the material you need to learn into manageable size and learn it, while at the same time reviewing the material that you already know.

Using the table above, any scores of 3 or below, you need to spend time learning, reviewing and practicing this subject area. A score of 4 means you need to review the material, but you don't have to re-learn it. A score of 5 and you are OK with just an occasional review before the exam.

A score of 0 or 1 means you really need to work on this area and should allocate the most time and the highest priority. Some students prefer a 5-day plan and others a 10-day plan. It also depends on how much time until the exam.

Here is an example of a 5-day plan based on an example from the table above:

> **Fractions:** 1 Study 1 hour everyday – review on last day
> **Science:** 3 Study 1 hour for 2 days then ½ hour a day, then review
> **Percent:** 4 Review every second day
> **Physics:** 2 Study 1 hour on the first day – then ½ hour everyday
> **Interpreting Written Material:** 5 Review for ½ hour every other day
> **Algebra:** 5 Review for ½ hour every other day
> **Decimals:** 5 very confident – review a few times.

Using this example, Algebra and Decimals are good, and only need occasional review. Science is also good and needs 'some' review. Decimals need a bit of work, Physics need a lot of work and Fractions are very weak and need the majority of time. Based on this, here is a sample study plan:

Day	Subject	Time
Monday		
Study	Fractions	1 hour
Study	Physics	1 hour
	½ hour break	
Study	Science	1 hour
Review	Decimals	½ hour
Tuesday		
Study	Fractions	1 hour
Study	Physics	½ hour
	½ hour break	
Study	Decimals	½ hour
Review	Percent	½ hour
Review	Decimals	½ hour
Wednesday		
Study	Fractions	1 hour
Study	Physics	½ hour
	½ hour break	
Study	Science	½ hour
Review	Decimals	½ hour
Thursday		
Study	Fractions	½ hour
Study	Physics	½ hour
Review	Science	½ hour
	½ hour break	
Review	Decimals	½ hour
Review	Percent	½ hour

Friday		
Review	Fractions	½ hour
Review	Physics	½ hour
Review	Science	½ hour
	½ hour break	
Review	Percent	½ hour
Review	Decimals	½ hour

Interpreting Specs, Codes & Manuals

Section Overview: This section contains two parts: Tutorials and a Self-Assessment.

The Tutorials are designed to review the general principles. Please note that these tutorials are not a complete literacy course; they assume a basic level of reading proficiency. If you find the material difficult to follow, we recommend seeking out additional basic reading instruction before proceeding.

The Self-Assessment contains questions designed to simulate the style and difficulty of the Skilled Trades Test. These are for skill practice only and are not identical to the official exam questions, which remain confidential.

The purpose of this Self-Assessment is to help you:

Identify your strengths and weaknesses.

Develop your personalized study plan.

Familiarize yourself with the test format.

Gain Experience: These questions act as a bonus "third practice test."

Establishing Your Baseline The self-assessment is designed to give you a baseline score. If you can master the questions below, you will be well-prepared for the this section of the actual test.

75% - 100%	Excellent – you have mastered the content
50 – 75%	Good. You have a working knowledge. Even though you can just pass this section, you may want to review the Tutorials and do some extra practice to see if you can improve your mark.
25% - 50%	Below Average. You do not understand the problems. Review the tutorials, and retake this quiz again in a few days, before proceeding to the rest of the practice test questions.
Less than 25%	Poor. You have a very limited understanding of the problems. Please review the tutorials, and retake this quiz again in a few days, before proceeding to the rest of the practice test questions.

After taking the Self-Assessment, use the table above to assess your understanding. If you scored low, read through the Tutorial,

INTERPRETING WRITTEN MATERIAL 17

Answer Sheet

	A	B	C	D
1	○	○	○	○
2	○	○	○	○
3	○	○	○	○
4	○	○	○	○
5	○	○	○	○
6	○	○	○	○
7	○	○	○	○
8	○	○	○	○

Material Safety Data Sheet (MSDS) for an industrial cleaning solvent used to remove grease from mechanical parts:

Product Use: Heavy-duty degreasing of metal components.
Hazard Identification: Liquid is flammable. Vapours may cause dizziness or irritation.
Protective Equipment: Safety goggles, nitrile gloves, and a respirator must be worn when working in areas with poor ventilation.

Handling & Storage:

- Keep container tightly closed when not in use.
- Store in a cool, dry, well-ventilated area away from open flames, welding work, or sparks.
- Do not use near heat sources above 40°C.
- Avoid prolonged inhalation of vapors.
- Emergency Procedures:
- If product contacts skin, wash thoroughly with soap and water.
- If inhaled and dizziness occurs, move the worker to fresh air immediately.
- In case of fire, use a Class B fire extinguisher only. Water may spread the flames.

Disposal: Follow local hazardous-waste disposal regulations. Do not pour product into drains or onto the ground.

1. According to the MSDS, which of the following actions is required when working with this product in an enclosed workspace?

    a. Wearing cotton gloves to avoid skin irritation

    b. Wearing a respirator to reduce inhalation of vapours

    c. Turning off ventilation systems to keep vapours contained

    d. Using water to control any small fires that may occur

2. Based on the "Handling & Storage" section, which situation would violate the safety guidelines?

a. Keeping the container sealed during breaks

b. Storing the product in a cool, ventilated room

c. Using the product near equipment that reaches 55°C

d. Wearing goggles and gloves while applying the solvent

3. A worker begins to feel dizzy while using the solvent. According to the MSDS, what should be done first?

a. Provide the worker with water to drink

b. Immediately move the worker to fresh air

c. Apply a cold compress to the worker's forehead

d. Report the incident to the supervisor before taking action

4. Why should the product NOT be disposed of by dumping it down a drain?

a. Because it will immediately harden and damage pipes

b. Because it may react with soap and create toxic fumes

c. Because it must be handled as hazardous waste

d. Because drains cannot carry liquids over 40°C

Lockout/Tagout Procedure for Electrical Panels

Before servicing or repairing any electrical panel, the worker must shut off the main power switch and apply an approved lock and identification tag.

1. Only authorized personnel may apply or remove locks.

2. After applying the lock, the worker must verify zero energy by testing the panel with an approved voltage tester.

3. The key to the lock must remain in the possession of the worker who applied it.

4. Once the repair is complete, the worker must remove tools, notify surrounding staff, and remove the lock and tag.

5. Power may only be restored after a final safety check.

5. According to the procedure, what must the worker do immediately after applying the lock?

    a. Restore power to confirm the breaker is working

    b. Test the panel to ensure there is no electrical energy

    c. Give the lock key to a supervisor for safekeeping

    d. Remove any tools left near the panel

6. Who is permitted to remove a lock from an electrical panel?

    a. Any worker who has completed safety training

    b. A supervisor only

    c. The worker who originally applied the lock

    d. Anyone assigned to finish the repair

7. Why must the key stay with the worker who applied the lock?

    a. To prevent someone else from unlocking the panel

    b. To ensure the supervisor can verify the key location

    c. Because the key is a shared tool that must be returned

    d. So the worker can lend it to others if needed

8. Which of the following steps must happen before power is restored?

    a. Removal of all other workers from the area

    b. Disconnecting the voltage tester

    c. A final safety check

    d. Testing the panel under load

Answer Key

1. B
Wearing a respirator to reduce inhalation of vapor

The MSDS clearly states that a respirator must be worn in areas with poor ventilation. Cotton gloves (A) are not listed, turning off ventilation (C) is dangerous, and water should not be used on fires (D).

2. C
Using the product near equipment that reaches 55°C

The document states the solvent should not be used near heat sources above 40°C, so 55°C violates the safety rule. The other options follow the MSDS guidelines.

3. B — Immediately move the worker to fresh air

The "Emergency Procedures" section specifies that if dizziness occurs after inhalation, move the person to fresh air.

The other options are not part of the official MSDS protocol and could delay proper action.

4. C
Because it must be handled as hazardous waste

The MSDS states disposal must follow hazardous-waste regulations. It does not say that it hardens (A), reacts with soap (B), or that drains cannot carry liquids over 40°C (D).

5. B
Step 2 requires verifying zero energy with a voltage tester.

6. C
Only the worker who applied the lock may remove it.

7. A
Keeping the key prevents unauthorized unlocking.

8. C
Power can only be restored after the final safety check.

Help with Interpreting Written Material

At first sight, written material tests look challenging especially if you are given long essays to answer only two to three questions. While reading, you might notice your attention waning, or feeling sleepy. Do not be discouraged because there are various tactics and long range strategies that make comprehending even long, boring essays easier.

Your friends before your foes. It is always best to start with essays or passages with familiar subjects rather than those with unfamiliar ones. This approach applies the same logic as tackling easy questions before hard ones. Skip passages that do not interest you and leave them for later.

Don't use 'special' reading techniques. This is not the time for speed-reading or anything like that – just plain ordinary reading – not too slow and not too fast.

Read through the entire passage and the questions before you do anything. Many students try reading the questions first and then looking for answers in the passage thinking this approach is more efficient. What these students do not realize is that it is often hard to navigate in unfamiliar roads. If you do not familiarize yourself with the passage first, looking for answers become not only time-consuming but also dangerous because you might miss the context of the answer you are looking for. If you read the questions first you will only confuse yourself and lose valuable time.

Familiarize yourself with these questions. If you are familiar with the common types of questions, you are able to take note of important parts of the passage, saving time. There are six major kinds of questions.

- **Main Idea**- Questions that ask for the central thought or significance of the passage.

- **Specific Details** - Questions that asks for explicitly stated ideas.

- **Drawing Inferences** - Questions that ask for a statement's intended meaning.

- **Context Meaning** – Questions that ask for the meaning of a word depending on the context.

- **Technique** – Questions that ask for the method of organization or the writing style of the author.

Read. Read. Read. The best preparation is always to read, read and read. If you are not used to reading lengthy passages, you will probably lose concentration. Increase your attention span by making a habit out of reading.

Interpreting written material becomes less daunting when you have trained yourself to read and understand fast. Always remember that it is easier to understand passages you are interested in. Do not read through passages hastily. Make mental notes of ideas you may be asked.

Interpreting Written Material Strategy

When facing this section of a standardized test, you need a strategy to be successful. You want to keep several steps in mind:

- First, make a note of the time and the number of sections. Time your work accordingly. Typically, four to five minutes per section is sufficient. Second, read the directions for each selection thoroughly before beginning (and listen well to any additional verbal instructions, as they will often clarify obscure or confusing written guidelines). You must know exactly how to do what you're about to do!

- Now you're ready to begin reading the selection. Read the passage carefully, noting significant characters or events on a scratch sheet of paper or underlining on the test sheet. Many students find making a basic list in the margins helpful. Quickly jot down or underline one-word summaries of characters, notable happenings, numbers, or key ideas. This will help you better retain information and focus wandering thoughts. Remember, however, that your main goal in doing this is to find the information that answers the questions. Even if you find the passage interesting, remember your goal and work fast but stay on track.

- Now read the question and all the choices. Now you have read the passage, have a general idea of the main ideas, and have marked the important points. Read the question and all the choices. Never choose an answer without reading them all! Questions are often designed to confuse – stay focussed and clear. Usually the answer choices will focus on one or two facts or inferences from the passage. Keep these clear in your mind.

- Search for the answer. With a very general idea of what the different choices are, go back to the passage and scan for the relevant information. Watch for big words, unusual or unique words. These make your job easier as you can scan the text for the particular word.

- Mark the Answer. Now you have the key information that the question is looking for. Go back to the question, quickly scan the choices and mark the correct one.

See the list above for the different types. Typically, there will be several questions dealing with facts from the selection, a couple more inference questions dealing with logical consequences of those facts, and periodically an application-oriented question surfaces to force you to make connections with what you already know. Some students prefer to answer the questions as listed, and feel classifying the question and then ordering is wasting precious time. Other students prefer to answer the different types of questions in order of how easy or difficult they are. The choice is yours and do whatever works for you. If you want to try answering in order of difficulty, here is a recommended order, answer fact questions first; they're easily found within the passage. Tackle inference problems next, after re-reading the question(s) as many times as you need to. Application or 'best guess' questions usually take the longest, so, save them for last.

Use the practice tests to try out both ways of answering and see what works for you.

For more help, see Multiple Choice Secrets at https://www.multiple-choice.ca.

Main Idea and Supporting Details

Identifying the main idea, topic and supporting details in a passage can feel like an overwhelming task. The passages used for standardized tests can be boring and seem difficult - Test writers don't use interesting passages or ones that talk about things most people are familiar with. Despite these obstacles, all passages and paragraphs will have the information you need to answer the questions.

The topic of a passage or paragraph is its subject. It's the general idea and can be summed up in a word or short phrase. On some standardized tests, there is a short description of the passage if it's taken from a longer work. Make sure you read the description as it might state the topic of the passage. If not, read the passage and ask yourself, "Who or what is this about?" For example:

> Over the years, school uniforms have been hotly debated. Arguments are made that students have the right to show individuality and express themselves by choosing their own clothes. However, this brings up social and academic issues. Some kids cannot afford to wear the clothes they like and might be bullied by the "better dressed" students. With attention drawn to clothes and the individual, students will lose focus on class work and the reason they are in school. School uniforms should be mandatory.

Ask: What is this paragraph about?

Topic: school uniforms

Once you have the topic, it's easier to find the main idea. The main idea is a specific statement telling what the writer wants you to understand about the topic. Writers usually state the main idea as a thesis statement. If you're looking for the main idea of a single paragraph, the main idea is called the topic sentence and will probably be the first or last sentence. If you're looking for the main idea of an entire passage, look for the thesis statement in either the first or last paragraph. The main idea is usually restated in the conclusion. To find the main idea of a passage or paragraph, follow these steps:

1. Find the topic.

2. Ask yourself, "What point is the author trying to make about the topic?"

3. Create your own sentence summarizing the author's point.

4. Look in the text for the sentence closest in meaning to yours.

Look at the example paragraph again. It's already established that the topic of the paragraph is school uniforms. What is the main idea/topic sentence?

Ask: "What point is the author trying to make about school uniforms?"

Summary: Students should wear school uniforms.

Topic sentence: School uniforms should be mandatory.

Main Idea: School uniforms should be mandatory.

Each paragraph offers supporting details to explain the main idea. The details could be facts or reasons, but they will always answer a question about the main idea. What? Where? Why? When? How? How much/many? Look at the example paragraph again. You'll notice that more than one sentence answers a question about the main idea. These are the supporting details.

Main Idea: School uniforms should be mandatory.

Ask: Why? Some kids cannot afford to wear clothes they like and could be bullied by the "better dressed" kids. Supporting Detail

With attention drawn to clothes and the individual, Students will lose focus on class work and the reason they are in school. Supporting Detail

What if the author doesn't state the main idea in a topic sentence? The passage will have an implied main idea. It's not as difficult to find as it might seem. Paragraphs are always organized around ideas. To find an implied main idea, you need to know the topic and then find the relationship between the supporting details. Ask yourself, "What is the point the author is making about the relationship between the details?."

> Cocoa is what makes chocolate good for you. Chocolate comes in many varieties. These delectable flavors include milk chocolate, dark chocolate, semi-sweet, and white chocolate.

Ask: What is this paragraph about?

Topic: Chocolate

Ask: What? Where? Why? When? How? How much/many?

Supporting details: Chocolate is good for you because it is made of cocoa, Chocolate is delicious, Chocolate comes in different delicious flavors

Ask: What is the relationship between the details and what is the author's point?

Main Idea: Chocolate is good because it is healthy and it tastes good.

Testing Tips for Main Idea Questions

1. Skim the questions – not the answer choices - before reading the passage.

2. Questions about main idea might use the words "theme," "generalization," or "purpose."

3. Save questions about the main idea for last. Questions can often be found in order in the passage.

3. Underline topic sentences in the passage. Most tests allow you to write in your test booklet.

4. Answer the question in your own words before looking at the answer choices. Then match your answer with an answer choice.

5. Cross out incorrect answer choices immediately to prevent confusion.

6. If two of the answer choices mean the same thing but use different words, they are BOTH incorrect.

7. If a question asks about the whole passage, cross out the answer choices that apply only to part of it.

8. If only part of the information is correct, that answer choice is incorrect.

9. An answer choice that is too broad is incorrect. All information needs to be backed up by the passage.

10. Answer choices with extreme wording are usually incorrect.

Drawing Inferences And Conclusions

Video Version of this Tutorial
https://www.test-preparation.ca/making-inferences/

Drawing inferences and making conclusions happens all the time. In fact, you probably do it every time you read—sometimes without even realizing it! For example, remember the first time you saw the movie "The Lion King." When you meet Scar for the first time, he is trapping a helpless mouse with his sharp claws preparing to eat it. When you see this action you guess that Scar is going to be a bad character in the movie. Nothing appeared to tell you this. No caption came across the bottom of the screen that said "Bad Guy." No red arrow pointed to Scar and said "Evil Lion." No, you made an inference about his character based on the context clue you were given. You do the same thing when you read!

When you draw an inference or make a conclusion you are doing the same thing, you are making an educated guess based on the hints the author gives you. We call these hints "context clues." Scar trapping the innocent mouse is the context clue about Scar's character.

Usually you are making inferences and drawing conclusions the entire time that you are reading. Whether you realize it or not, you are constantly making educated guesses based on context clues. Think about a time you were reading a book and something happened that you were expecting to happen. You're not psychic! Actually, you were picking up on the context clues and making inferences about what was going to happen next!

Let's try an easy example. Read the following sentences and answer the questions at the end of the passage.

Shelly really likes to help people. She loves her job because she gets to help people every single day. However, Shelly has to work long hours and she can get called in the middle of the night for emergencies. She wears a white lab coat at work and usually she carries a stethoscope.

What is most likely Shelly's job?

    a. Musician

    b. Lawyer

    c. Doctor

    d. Teacher

This probably seemed easy. Drawing inferences isn't always this simple, but it is the same basic principle. How did you know Shelly was a doctor? She helps people, she works long hours, she wears a white lab coat, and she gets called in for emergencies at night. Context Clues! Nowhere in the paragraph did it say Shelly was a doctor, but you were able to draw that conclusion based on the information provided in the paragraph. This is how it's done!

There is a catch, though. Remember that when you draw inferences based on reading, you should only use the information given to you by the author. Sometimes it is easy for us to make conclusions based on knowledge that is already in our mind—but that can lead you to drawing an incorrect inference. For example, let's pretend there is a bully at your school named Brent. Now let's say you read a story and the main character's name is Brent. You could NOT infer that the character in the story is a bully just because his name is Brent. You should only use the information given to you by the author to avoid drawing the wrong conclusion.

Let's try another example. Read the passage below and answer the question.

Social media is an extremely popular new form of connecting and communicating over the internet. Since Facebook's original launch in 2004, millions of people have joined in the social media craze. In fact, it is estimated that almost 75% of all internet users aged 18 and older use some form of social media. Facebook started at Harvard University as a way to get students connected. However, it quickly grew into a worldwide phenomenon and today, the founder of Facebook, Mark Zuckerberg has an estimated net worth of 28.5 billion dollars.

Facebook is not the only social media platform, though. Other sites such as Twitter, Instagram, and Snapchat have since been invented and are quickly becoming just as popular! Many social media users actually use more than one type of social media. Furthermore, most social media sites have created mobile apps that allow people to connect via social media virtually anywhere in the world!

What is the most likely reason that other social media sites like Twitter and Instagram were created?

    a. Professors at Harvard University made it a class project.

    b. Facebook was extremely popular and other people thought they could also be successful by designing social media sites.

    c. Facebook was not connecting enough people.

    d. Mark Zuckerberg paid people to invent new social media sites because he wanted lots of competition.

Here, the correct answer is B. Facebook was extremely popular and other people thought they could also be successful by designing social media sites. How do we know this? What are the context clues? Take a look at the first paragraph. What do we know based on this paragraph? Well, one sentence refers to Facebook's original launch. This suggests that Facebook was one of the first social media sites. In addition, we know that the founder of Facebook has been extremely successful and is worth billions of dollars. From this we can infer that other people wanted to imitate Facebook's idea and become just as successful as Mark Zuckerberg.

Let's go through the other answers. If you chose A, it might be because Facebook started at Harvard University, so you drew the conclusion that all other social media sites were also started at Harvard University. However, there is no mention of class projects, professors, or students designing social media. So there doesn't seem to be enough support for choice A.

If you chose C, you might have been drawing your own conclusions based on outside information. Maybe none of your friends are on Facebook, so you made an inference that

Facebook didn't connect enough people, so more sites were invented. Or maybe you think the people who connect on Facebook are too old, so you don't think Facebook connects enough people your age. This might be true, but remember inferences should be drawn from the information the author gives you!

If you chose D, you might be using the information that Mark Zuckerberg is worth over 28 billion dollars. It would be easy for him to pay others to design new sites, but remember, you need to use context clues! He is very wealthy, but that statement was giving you information about how successful Facebook was—not suggesting that he paid others to design more sites!

So remember, drawing inferences and conclusions is simply about using the information you are given to make an educated guess. You do this every single day so don't let this concept scare you. Look for the context clues, make sure they support your claim, and you'll be able to make accurate inferences and conclusions!

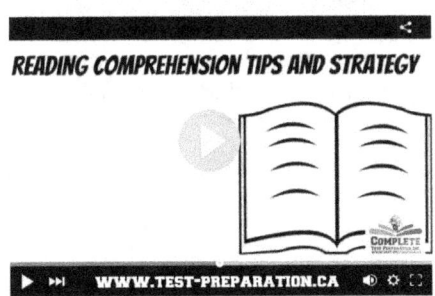 

TOOLBOX MATH

Section Overview: Mathematics & Trade Math This section contains two parts: Mathematics Tutorials and a Self-Assessment.

The Tutorials are designed to review the specific mathematical principles and formulas used in the skilled trades. Please note that these tutorials are not a comprehensive math course; they assume a foundational understanding of basic arithmetic (addition, subtraction, multiplication, and division). If you struggle with these core concepts, we recommend seeking out basic adult education resources to build your foundation before proceeding.

The Self-Assessment contains questions designed to simulate the style, difficulty, and content of the Skilled Trades Test.

The purpose of this Self-Assessment is to help you:

Identify your mathematical strengths and weaknesses.

Develop a personalized study plan to target problem areas.

Familiarize yourself with the way math questions are worded on the exam.

Gain Experience: Use this as a bonus "third practice test."

Establishing Your Baseline The self-assessment is designed to give you a baseline score. If you can master the questions below, you will be well-prepared for the Mathematics section of the actual test.

75% - 100%	Excellent – you have mastered the content
50 – 75%	Good. You have a working knowledge. Even though you can just pass this section, you may want to review the tutorials and do some extra practice to see if you can improve your mark.
25% - 50%	Below Average. You do not understand the content. Review the tutorials, and retake this quiz again in a few days, before proceeding to the rest of the practice test questions.
Less than 25%	Poor. You have a very limited understanding. Please review the Tutorials, and retake this quiz again in a few days, before proceeding to the rest of the practice test questions.

Toolbox Math Self-Assessment

	A	B	C	D
1	○	○	○	○
2	○	○	○	○
3	○	○	○	○
4	○	○	○	○
5	○	○	○	○
6	○	○	○	○
7	○	○	○	○
8	○	○	○	○
9	○	○	○	○
10	○	○	○	○
11	○	○	○	○
12	○	○	○	○
13	○	○	○	○
14	○	○	○	○
15	○	○	○	○
16	○	○	○	○
17	○	○	○	○
18	○	○	○	○
19	○	○	○	○
20	○	○	○	○

Toolbox Math

Part 1: Whole Numbers & Operations

1. A construction site requires 485 bricks for a retaining wall. If the bricks are delivered in pallets of 60, how many full pallets must be ordered to ensure there are enough bricks?

    a. 8
    b. 8.08
    c. 9
    d. 7

2. An electrician installs 14 outlets on the first floor, 19 on the second floor, and 12 in the basement. If each outlet takes 15 minutes to install, how many minutes total will the installation take?

    a. 45 minutes
    b. 600 minutes
    c. 675 minutes
    d. 725 minutes

3. Evaluate the following expression using the order of operations: 12 + (8 X 5) - 10 \ 2

    a. 47
    b. 95
    c. 20
    d. 55

4. A plumber buys 500 feet of PEX piping. He uses 125 feet for the first job, 210 feet for the second job, and 45 feet for the third. How many feet of piping remain?

    a. 380 feet
    b. 120 feet
    c. 220 feet
    d. 880 feet

5. A crate of tools weighs 145 lbs. If a forklift can carry 1,800 lbs, how many full crates can it carry at one time safely?

    a. 11
    b. 12
    c. 12.4
    d. 13

Part 2: Fractions & Decimals

6. A carpenter needs to cut a board to 15 3/8 inches. The board is currently 18 1/2 inches long. How much needs to be cut off?

    a. 3 1/8 inches
    b. 3 1/4 inches
    c. 2 7/8 inches
    d. 3 1/2 inches

7. Convert 0.625 into a fraction in its simplest form.

    a. 3/5
    b. 5/8
    c. 2/3
    d. 6/10

8. Which of the following is the largest drill bit size?

   a. 3/8 inch
   b. 5/16 inch
   c. 1/2
   d. 7/16

9. A welder joins two steel plates. One plate is 0.375 inches thick, and the other is 0.125 inches thick. What is the total combined thickness?

   a. 0.50 inches
   b. 0.49 inches
   c. 0.55 inches
   d. 0.40 inches

10. You need to divide a 5 1/4 foot pipe into 3 equal sections. How long is each section?

    a. 1/2
    b. 1/4
    c. 3/4
    d. 2 feet

Part 3: Ratios, Proportions & Percentages

11. A concrete mix requires a ratio of 1 part cement to 3 parts sand. If you have 40 kg of sand, how much cement do you need (rounded to the nearest whole number)?

    a. 10 kg
    b. 12 kg
    c. 13 kg
    d. 15 kg

12. A contractor estimates a job will cost $4,500. If he adds a 15% contingency fee for unexpected costs, what is the new total estimate?

   a. $5,000
   b. $4,675
   c. $5,175
   d. $6,750

13. Gear A has 12 teeth and turns Gear B, which has 36 teeth. What is the ratio of teeth from Gear A to Gear B in simplest form?

   a. 1:2
   b. 1:3
   c. 3:1
   d. 1:4

14. A 50-gallon tank is 20% full. How many gallons are currently in the tank?

   a. 5 gallons
   b. 10 gallons
   c. 15 gallons
   d. 20 gallons

15. If 2 painters can paint a room in 6 hours, how many hours would it take for 3 painters to paint the same room (assuming they work at the same pace)?

   a. 3 hours
   b. 4 hours
   c. 5 hours
   d. 9 hours

Part 4: Measurement & Geometry

16. How many inches are in 6 feet 4 inches?

    a. 72 inches

    b. 76 inches

    c. 64 inches

    d. 78 inches

17. Calculate the area of a rectangular workshop floor that measures 12 feet by 15 feet.

    a. 54 sq ft

    b. 160 sq ft

    c. 180 sq ft

    d. 27 sq ft

18. What is the perimeter of a square room with a side length of 14 feet?

    a. 28 feet

    b. 56 feet

    c. 196 feet

    d. 42 feet

19. A cylindrical water tank has a diameter of 4 meters. What is the radius?

    a. 2 meters

    b. 4 meters

    c. 8 meters

    d. 12.56 meters

20. A room volume is calculated by L X W X H. If a room is 10 ft long, 8 ft wide, and 8 ft high, what is the volume?

    a. 640 cubic ft

    b. 160 cubic ft

    c. 800 cubic ft

    d. 64 cubic ft

Answer Key & Solutions

1. C 9
Step 1: Divide total bricks needed by bricks per pallet: 485 \60 = 8.0833
Step 2: You cannot order 0.08 of a pallet. You must round up to the next whole number to ensure you have enough.
Step 3: Round 8.08 up to 9.

2. C 675 minutes
Step 1: Calculate total outlets: 14 + 19 + 12 = 45 outlets.
Step 2: Multiply total outlets by time per outlet: 45 X 15 mins/outlet.
Step 3: 45 X 15 = 675.

3. A 47
Step 1 (Parentheses): Solve 8 X 5 = 40. The equation is now 12 + 40 - 10 \ 2.
Step 2 (Division): Solve 10 / 2 = 5. The equation is now 12 + 40 - 5.
Step 3 (Add/Subtract left to right): 12 + 40 = 52.
Step 4: 52 - 5 = 47.

4. B 120 feet
Step 1: Add up the used piping: 125 + 210 + 45 = 380 feet used.
Step 2: Subtract used amount from total: 500 - 380 = 120 feet remaining.

5. B 12
Step 1: Divide the forklift capacity by the crate weight: 1,800 / 145 = 12.41.
Step 2: The forklift cannot safely carry the 0.41 portion of a 13th crate (that would exceed the weight limit).
Step 3: Round down to the nearest whole number: 12.

6. A 3 1/8
Step 1: Set up the subtraction: 18 1/2 - 15 3/8}.
Step 2: Find a common denominator for the fractions. The common denominator for 2 and 8 is 8.
Step 3: Convert 1/2 to eighths: (1 X 4)/ (2 X 4} = 4/8.
Step 4: Now subtract: 18 4/8 - 15 3/8}.
Step 5: Subtract whole numbers (18 - 15 = 3) then fractions (4/8 - 3/8 = 1/8. Result: 3 1/8.

7. B 5/8
Step 1: Write the decimal as a fraction over 1000 (since there are 3 decimal places): 625/1000.
Step 2: Simplify by dividing top and bottom by 25: 25/40.
Step 3: Simplify again by dividing by 5: 5/8.

8. C 1/2
Step 1: Convert all fractions to a common denominator (16 is the easiest common denominator here).
Step 2:
- 3/8 = 6/16
- 5/16 = 5/16
- 1/2 = 8/16
- 7/16 = 7/16

Step 3: Compare numerators. 8 is the largest, so 1/2 is the largest bit.

9. A 0.50 inches
Step 1: Align the decimal points:

0.375
0.125

Step 2: Add starting from the right: 5 + 5 = 10 (carry the 1), 7 + 2 + 1 = 10 (carry the 1), 3 + 1 + 1 = 5.
Step 3: Result is 0.500 or 0.50.

10. C 1 3/4
Step 1: Convert mixed number to improper fraction.
5 1/4 = (5 X 4) + 1/4 = 21/4.
Step 2: Divide by 3. 21/4 / 3 = 21/4 X 1/3.
Step 3: Multiply: 21 X 1/4 X 3 = 21/12.
Step 4: Simplify 21/12. Divide top and bottom by 3: 7/4.
Step 5: Convert back to mixed number: 4 goes into 7 once, with 3 remainder. Result: 1 3/4.

11. C 13 kg
Step 1: The ratio is 1 (Cement) : 3 (Sand).
Step 2: Set up the proportion: 1/3 = X (Cement)/40 (Sand).
Step 3: Cross multiply: 3x = 40.
Step 4: Solve for x: 40 / 3 = 13.33.
Step 5: Round to nearest whole number: 13 kg.

12. C $5,175
Step 1: Convert percentage to decimal: 15% = 0.15.
Step 2: Calculate the contingency amount:
$4,500 X 0.15 = 675.
Step 3: Add to the original cost: 4,500 + 675 = 5,175.

13. B 1:3
Step 1: Write the ratio as 12:36.
Step 2: Divide both numbers by the greatest common divisor (12).
Step 3: 12 / 12 = 1; 36 / 12 = 3. Result: 1:3.

14. B 10 gallons
Step 1: Convert percentage to decimal: 20% = 0.20.
Step 2: Multiply total capacity by the decimal:
50 X 0.20.
Step 3: 50 X 0.2 = 10.

15. B 4 hours
Step 1: Calculate "Man-Hours" needed for the job.
2 painters X 6 hours = 12 Man-Hours total work.
Step 2: Divide total Man-Hours by the new number of workers (3).
Step 3: 12 Man-Hours / 3 painters = 4 hours.

16. B 76 inches
Step 1: Know the conversion: 1 foot = 12 inches.
Step 2: Convert feet to inches: 6 feet X 12 = 72 inches.
Step 3: Add the extra inches: 72 + 4 = 76 inches.

17. C 180 sq ft
Step 1: Formula for Area of a rectangle =
Length times Width.
Step 2: 12 X 15.
Step 3: 12 times 10 = 120; 12 times 5 = 60; 120 + 60 = 180.
Result: 180 sq ft.

18. B 56 feet
Step 1: Formula for Perimeter of a square =
4 X Side.
Step 2: 4 X 14.
Step 3: = 56 feet.

19. A 2 meters
Step 1: Know the relationship: Radius is half of the Diameter
r = d/2.
Step 2: 4 / 2 = 2.

20. A 640 cubic ft
Step 1: Formula for Volume =
Length X Width X Height.
Step 2: First multiply Length X Width: 10 X 8 = 80.
Step 3: Multiply result by Height: 80 X 8 = 640.

Basic Math Video Tutorials

https://www.test-preparation.ca/math-videos/

Fraction Tips, Tricks and Shortcuts

When you are writing an exam, time is precious, so anything you can do to answer questions faster is a real advantage.

Here are some ideas, shortcuts, tips and tricks that can speed up answering fraction problems.

Remember that a fraction is just a number which names a portion of something. For instance, instead of having a whole pie, a fraction says you have a part of a pie--such as a half of one or a fourth of one.

Two numbers make up a fraction. The number on top is the numerator. The number on the bottom is the denominator.

To remember which is which, just remember that "denominator" and "down" both start with a "d." And the "downstairs" number is the denominator. So for instance, in ½, the numerator is 1, and the denominator (or "downstairs") number is 2.

Adding Fractions

It's easy to add two fractions if they have the same denominator. Just add the digits on top and leave the bottom one the same: 1/10 + 6/10 = 7/10.

It's the same with subtracting fractions with the same denominator: 7/10 - 6/10 = 1/10.

Adding and subtracting fractions with different denominators is more complicated.

First, you have to arrange the fractions so they have the same denominators.

The easiest way to do this is to multiply the denominators: For 2/5 + 1/2 multiply 5 by 2. Now you have a denominator of 10.

But now you have to change the top numbers too. Since you multiplied the 5 in 2/5 by 2, you also multiply the 2 by 2, to get 4. So the first fraction is now 4/10.

In the second fraction, you multiplied the denominator by 5, you have to multiply the numerator by 5 also, to get 5/10.

Now you have 4/10 + 5/10 and you can add 5 and 4 to get 9/10.

Simplest Form

To reduce a fraction to its simplest form, you have to arrange the numerator and denominator so the only common factor is 1.

Think of it this way:

Let's take an example: The fraction 2/10.

This is not reduced to its simplest terms because there is a number that will divide evenly into both: 2. We want to make it so that the only number that will divide evenly into both is 1.

Divide the top and bottom by 2 to get the new, reduced fraction - 1/5.

Multiplying Fractions

This is the easiest of all: Just multiply the two top numbers and then multiply the two bottom numbers.

Here is an example,

2/5 X 2/3

First, multiply the numerators: 2 X 2 = 4

then multiply the denominators: 5 X 3 = 15

Your answer is 4/15.

Dividing Fractions

Dividing fractions is easy if you remember a simple trick - first turn the second fraction upside down - then multiply!

Here is an example:

7/8 X 1/2

Turn the second fraction upside down:

7/8 X 2/1

then multiply:

(7 X 2) / (8 X 1) = 14/8

Converting Fractions to Decimals

There are a couple of ways to convert fractions to decimals. The first, which is the fastest -- is to memorize some basic fraction facts.

1/100 is "one hundredth," expressed as a decimal, it's .01.

    1/50 is "two hundredths," expressed as a decimal, it's .02.

    1/25 is "one twenty-fifth" or "four hundredths," expressed as a decimal, it's .04.

    1/20 is "one twentieth" or ""five hundredths," expressed as a decimal, it's .05.

    1/10 is "one tenth," expressed as a decimal, it's .1.

    1/8 is "one eighth," or "one hundred twenty-five thousandths," expressed as a decimal, it's .125.

    1/5 is "one fifth," or "two tenths," expressed as a decimal, it's .2.

    1/4 is "one fourth" or "twenty-five hundredths," expressed as a decimal, it's .25.

    1/3 is "one third" or "thirty-three hundredths," expressed as a decimal, it's .33.

    1/2 is "one half" or "five tenths," expressed as a decimal, it's .5.

    3/4 is "three fourths," or "seventy-five hundredths," expressed as a decimal, it's .75.

Of course, if you're no good at memorization, another good technique for converting a fraction to a decimal is to manipulate it so that the fraction's denominator is 10, 100, 1000, or some other power of 10.

Here's an example: We'll start with three quarters. What is the first number in the 4 "times table" that you can multiply and get a multiple of 10? Can you multiply 4 by something to get 10? No. Can you multiply it by something to get 100? Yes! 4 X 25 is 100.

So multiply the numerator by 25, which is 75 over 100

We know fractions are really a division problem, and we also know that dividing by 100, means we move the decimal 2 places to the left.

So, 75 over 100 = .75

Lets try another example - Convert one fifth to a decimal.

First find a power of 10 that 5 goes into evenly, which is 2.

Multiply the numerator and denominator by 2, which is

two tenths.

Dividing 2 by 10 means we move the decimal place 1 place to the left.

So one fifth = zero point two

Converting Fractions to Percent

Here is a quick method to convert fraction to percent and a strategy for answering on a multiple choice test that will save you valuable exam time.

First, remember that a fraction is a division problem: you're dividing the bottom number into the top.

Taking an example, convert 2/3 into percent.

The first method is to multiple the numerator by 100 and divide. So,

(2 X 100) / 2 = 100/3 = 66.66

Add a % sign and you have the answer, 66.66%

If you're doing these conversions on a multiple-choice test, here's an idea that might be even easier and faster. Let's say you have a fraction of 1/8 and you're asked to convert to percent.
Since we know that "percent" means hundredths, ask yourself what number we can multiply 8 by to get 100. Since

there is no number, ask what number gets us close to 100.

That number is 12: 8 X 12 = 96. So it gets us a little less than 100. Now, whatever you do to the denominator, you have to do to the numerator. Let's multiply 1 X 12 and we get 12. However, since 96 is a little less than 100, we know that our answer will be a little MORE than 12%.

Look at the choices and eliminate the obvious wrong choices. So if your possible answers on the multiple-choice test are these:

a) 8.5% b) 19% c) 12.5% d) 25%

then we know the answer is c) 12.5%, because it's a little MORE than the 12 we got in our math problem above.

Here all the choices except choice C 12.5% can be eliminated.

You don't have to know the exact correct answer, just enough to estimate, then eliminate the obviously wrong answers.

This was an easy example to demonstrate the strategy, but don't be fooled! You probably won't get such an easy question on your exam. By estimating your answer quickly, then eliminating obviously incorrect choices immediately, you save precious exam time.

Decimal Tips, Tricks and Short-cuts

CONVERTING DECIMALS TO FRACTIONS

Converting decimals to fractions is easy if you say it the right way! If you say "point one" or "point 25," you'll have trouble.

But if you say, "one tenth" and "twenty-five hundredths," then you have already solved it! That's because, if you know your fractions, you know that "one tenth" looks like this: 1/10. And "twenty-five hundredths" looks like this: 25/100.

Even if you have digits before the decimal, such as 3.4, learning how to say the word will help you with the conversion into a fraction. It's not "three point four," it's "three and four tenths." Knowing this, you know that the fraction which looks like "three and four tenths" is 3 4/10.

The conversion is not complete until you reduce the fraction to its lowest terms: It's not 25/100, but 1/4.

Converting Decimals to Percent

Changing a decimal to a percent is easy if you remember one thing: multiply by 100.

For example, if you start with .45, simply multiply it by 100 for 45. Then add the % sign to the end - 45%.

Think of it this way: take out the decimal point, add a percent sign on the opposite side. In other words, the decimal on the left is replaced by the % on the right.

It doesn't work quite that easily if the decimal is in the middle of the number. For example, 3.7. Here, take out the decimal in the middle and replace it with a 0 % at the end. So 3.7 converted to decimal is 370%.

Percent Tips, Tricks and Shortcuts

Percent problems are not nearly as scary as they appear, if you remember this neat trick:

Draw a cross as in:

Portion	Percent
Whole	100

In the upper left, write PORTION. In the bottom left, write WHOLE. In the top right, write PERCENT and in the bottom right, write 100. Whatever your problem is, you will leave blank the unknown, and fill in the other four parts. For example, let's suppose your problem is: Find 10% of 50. Since we know the 10% part, we put 10 in the percent corner. Since the whole number in our problem is 50, we put that in the corner marked whole. You always put 100 underneath the percent, so we leave it as is, which leaves only the top left corner blank. This is where we'll put our answer. Now simply multiply the two corner numbers that are NOT 100. Here, it's 10 X 50. That gives us 500. Now divide this by the remaining corner, or 100, to get a final answer of 5. 5 is the number that goes in the upper-left corner, and is your final solution.

Another hint to remember: Percents are the same thing as hundredths in decimals. So .45 is the same as 45 hundredths or 45 percent.

Converting Percents to Decimals

Percents are just a type of decimal, so it should be no surprise that converting between the two is actually fairly simple. Here are a few tricks and shortcuts to keep in mind:

- ☐ Remember that percent literally means "per 100" or "for every 100." So when you speak of 30% you're saying 30 for every 100 or the fraction 30/100. In basic math, you learned that fractions that have 10 or 100 as the denominator can easily be turned to a decimal. 30/100 is thirty hundredths, or expressed as a decimal, .30.

- Another way to look at it: To convert a percent to a decimal, simply divide the number by 100. So for instance, if the percent is 47%, divide 47 by 100. The result will be .47. Get rid of the % mark and you're done.
- Remember that the easiest way of dividing by 100 is by moving your decimal two spots to the left.

Converting Percent to Fractions

Converting Percent to Fractions is easy. After all, a percent is just a type of fraction; it tells you what part of 100 that you're talking about. Here are some simple ideas for making the conversion from a percent to a fraction:

- If the percent is a whole number -- say 34% -- then simply write a fraction with 100 as the denominator (the bottom number). Then put the percentage itself on top. So 34% becomes 34/100.
- Now reduce as you would reduce any percent. Here, by dividing 2 into 34 and 2 into 100, you get 17/50.
- If your percent is not a whole number -- say 3.4% --then convert it to a decimal expressed as hundredths. 3.4 is the same as 3.40 (or 3 and forty hundredths). Now ask yourself how you would express "three and forty hundredths" as a fraction. It would, of course, be 3 40/100. Reduce this and it becomes 3 2/5.

Exponents: Tips, Shortcuts & Tricks

Exponents are just shorthand for saying that you're multiplying a number by itself two or more times.

For instance, instead of saying 5 x 5 x 5, you can show that you're multiplying 5 by itself 3 times if you just write 5^3.

We usually say this as "five to the third power" or "five to the power of three." In this example, the raised 3 is an "exponent," and the 5 is the "base."

You can even use exponents with fractions. For instance, $1/2^3$ means you're multiplying 1/2 x 1/2 x 1/2. (The answer is 1/8).

Multiplying Exponents

For exponents with the same base, for instance 5^3 X 5^2, add the exponents on the same base. The answer, then, is 5^5.

If the bases are different, for example, in 5^3 X 3^2, you have to do the math the long way to figure it out.

5 x 5 x 5 = 125, and 3 X 3 = 9.

125 X 9 = 1125

Dividing Exponents

For exponents with the same base, subtract the exponents. In the problem above, 5^3 X 5^2, 3 - 2 = 1. 5 to the power of 1 is 5.

Here are some Quick things to remember

Any number to the power of 1 is that number.

Any number raised to the power of 0 is 1.

Number (x)	x^2	x^3
1	1	1
2	4	8
3	9	27
4	16	64
5	25	125
6	36	216
7	49	343
8	64	512
9	81	729
10	100	1000

How to Answer Basic Math Multiple Choice

The time allowed on the math portion of a standardized test is typically so short that there's no room for error. You have to be fast and accurate.

Math strategy is very helpful, but nothing beats knowing your stuff! Make sure that you have learned all the important formulas that will be used.

If you don't know the formulas, strategy won't help you.

How to Answer Basic Math Questions - the Basics

First, read the problem, but not the answers.

Work through the problem first and come up with your own answers. Hopefully, you should find your answer among the choices.

If no answer matches the one you got, re-check your math, but this time, use a different method. In math, there are different ways to solve a problem.

Math Multiple Choice Strategy

The two strategies for working with basic math multiple choice are Estimation and Elimination.

Estimation is just as it sounds - try to estimate an approximate answer first. Then look at the choices.

Elimination is probably the most powerful strategy for answering multiple choice.

Eliminate obviously incorrect answers and narrowing the possible choices.

Here are a few basic math examples of how this works.

Solve 2/3 + 5/12

    a. 9/17

    b. 3/11

    c. 7/12

    d. 1 1/12

First estimate the answer. 2/3 is more than half and 5/12 is about half, so the answer is going to be very close to 1.

Next, Eliminate. Choice A is about 1/2 and can be eliminated, choice B is very small, less than 1/2 and can be eliminated. Choice C is close to 1/2 and can be eliminated. Leaving only choice D, which is just over 1.

Work through the solution, find a common denominator and add. The correct answer is 1 1/12, so Choice D is correct.

Let's look at another example:

Solve 4/5 – 2/3

    a. 2/2
    b. 2/13
    c. 1
    d. 2/15

First, quickly estimate the answer. 4/5 is very close to 1, and 2/3 more than half, so the answer is going to be less than 1/2.

Choice A can be eliminated right away, because it is 1. Choice C can be eliminated for the same reason.

Next, look at the denominators. Since 5 and 3 don't go into 13, choice B can be eliminated as well.

That leaves choice D. Checking the answer, the common denominator will be 15. So the answer is 2/15 and choice D is correct.

Fractions shortcut - Cancelling out.

In any operation with fractions, if the numerator of one fraction has a common multiple with the denominator of the other, you can cancel out. This saves time, and simplifies the problem quickly, making it easier to manage.

Solve 2/15 ÷ 4/5

    a. 6/65

    b. 6/75

    c. 5/12

    d. 1/6

To divide fractions, we multiply the first fraction with the inverse of the second fraction. Therefore we have 2/15 x 5/4. The numerator of the first fraction, 2, shares a multiple with the denominator of the second fraction, 4, which is 2. These cancel out, which gives, 1/3 x 1/2 = 1/6

Cancelling Out solved the questions very quickly, but we can still use multiple choice strategies to answer.

Choice B can be eliminated because 75 is too large a denominator. Choice C can be eliminated because 5 and 15 don't go into 12.

Choice D is correct.

Decimal Multiple Choice Strategy and Shortcuts.

Multiplying decimals gives a very quick way to estimate and eliminate choices. Anytime that you multiply decimals, it is going to give an answer with the same number of decimal places as the combined operands.

So for example,

2.38 X 1.2 will produce a number with three places of decimal, which is 2.856.

Here are a few examples with step-by-step explanation:

Solve 2.06 x 1.2

    a. 24.82

    b. 2.482

    c. 24.72

    d. 2.472

This is a simple question, but even before you start calculating, you can eliminate several choices. When multiplying decimals, there will always be as many numbers behind the decimal place in the answer as the sum of the ones in the initial problem, so choices A and C can be eliminated.

The correct answer is D: 2.06 x 1.2 = 2.472

Solve 20.0 ÷ 2.5

    a. 12.05

    b. 9.25

    c. 8.3

    d. 8

First estimate the answer to be around 10, and eliminate choice A. And since it'd also be an even number, you can eliminate Choices B and C, leaving only choice D.

The correct answer is D: 20.0 ÷ 2.5 = 8

Order Of Operation

Some math calculations contain more than one set of operations. For example, a problem like 3 + (35 - 21) x 2 requires addition, subtraction and multiplication operations. The problem arises from the confusion of which of the operations to perform first. Starting with the wrong operation will give you the wrong answer. To solve this dilemma and to avoid confusion, the Order of Operation rules were set.

Order of operation is a set of mathematical rules designed to be used for calculations that require more than one arithmetic operation. For example, calculation problems that require two or more out of addition, subtraction, multiplication and division, would require that you follow the order of operation to solve.

The order of operation rules are quite simple as explained below.

Rule 1:   Start with calculations that are inside brackets or parentheses.
Rule 2:   Then, solve all multiplications and divisions, from left to right.
Rule 3:   Finally, solve all additions and subtractions, from left to right.

Example 1

Solve 16 + 5 x 8

Based on the rules above, we would have to start with the multiplication part of the question.
That will give: 16 + 40 = 56

Take note that if the rule was not followed and addition was done first, the answer gotten would be different and wrong.

16 + 5 x 8
21 x 8 = 168 (wrong answer)

Example 2

3 +(35 - 21) x 2

Based on the rules of the order of operation, we have to solve the problem in the bracket or parenthesis first. Then we do the multiplication, before doing the addition.

3 + (35 - 21) x 2

3 + (14) x 2
3 + 28
= 31

Classroom to Job Site: The "Shop Math" Translator

How to Convert Word Problems into Trade Formulas (Imperial & Metric)

Most apprentices don't fail the math section because they can't push buttons on a calculator. They fail because they don't know which buttons to push.

In high school, the teacher gave you the formula: A = L times W.

On the job site (and on the STAR test), you get a sentence:

"Determine the total flooring required for the hallway, allowing for 10% wastage."

There is no "wastage" button on your calculator. You need to translate English into Math. This chapter is your dictionary.

Part 1: The Trade Math "Dictionary"

When you read a question, stop looking for the numbers. Look for the Action Words. These words tell you exactly which operation to perform.

The "Addition" Words (+)

"Total length or Total weight" → Add everything up.
"Combined" → Put two or more measurements together.
"Perimeter" → Add all the sides of the shape.
"Include" → Add this number to your running total.

The "Subtraction" Words (-)
"Difference" → Big number minus small number.
"Remaining" → What is left after you take something away.
"Clearance or Gap" → Subtract the thickness of the material or the required space.
"Tolerance" → The allowable variation (usually ±, meaning add AND subtract to find the range).
"Deduction" → Often used in sheet metal (bend allowance) or plumbing (fitting allowance).

The "Multiplication" Words (X, or *)
"OF" → This is the most important word in trade math. "Of" almost always means multiply.

Example: "50% of the load" means 0.50 times L.

"Area" → Length X Width.
"Volume" → Length X Width X Height.
"Sets / Rows / Layers" → Multiply the item count by the number of sets.

The "Division" Words (\)
"Per" → Used when splitting things up.

Example: "Cost per foot" means Total Cost \ Total Feet.

"On Center (O.C.)" → Divide the total length by the spacing.
"Ratio" → A comparison (e.g., slope is Rise \ Run).
"Average" → Total Sum \ Number of Items.

Part 2: The "Wastage" Trap (And How to Fix It)

The most common "trick" question on trade exams involves calculating materials with waste.

The Amateur Way:
1. Calculate the exact area.
2. Calculate 10% of that area.
3. Add the two numbers together.

This works, but it is slow and prone to errors.

The Pro Way (The "1.X" Multiplier):
If you need to add a percentage, put a "1" in front of the percentage and multiply.
"Allow for 10% wastage" → Multiply total by 1.10
"Allow for 15% wastage" → Multiply total by 1.15
"Add 5% for cuts" → Multiply total by 1.05
"Include 12% tax" → Multiply price by 1.12

Example: You need 500 sq. ft. of hardwood. Allow 10% for waste.
Formula: 500 X 1.10 = 550 sq. ft.
Done in one step!

Part 3: The Canadian Context (Metric vs. Imperial)

Canada is unique. We design buildings in Metric (millimeters), but we buy materials in Imperial (feet and inches). A 2 x 4 is not measured in centimeters, and a sheet of plywood is 4'x 8'.

To pass the STAR test, and to survive on a job site, you must be "bilingual" in measurement.

The "Big Three" Conversions
Memorize these. Do not rely on looking them up every time.
1. The Inch-to-Millimeter Bridge

The Golden Number: 25.4
Imperial to Metric: Multiply by 25.4

Example: 2 inches times 25.4 = 50.8 mm

Metric to Imperial: Divide by 25.4

Example: 100 mm / 25.4 = 3.937 inches

2. The Feet-to-Meter Bridge
The Golden Number: 3.28 (approximate) or 0.3048 (exact)

Quick Check: A meter is slightly longer than a yard (3 feet).

Meters to Feet: Multiply by 3.28

Example: 10 meters times 3.28 = 32.8 feet

3. The Weight Bridge (Mass)
The Golden Number: 2.2

Kilograms to Pounds: Multiply by 2.2

Example: A 25kg bag of cement. 25 times 2.2 = 55 lbs.

Crucial Test Tip: "Apples to Apples"
Never calculate area or volume using mixed units.

WRONG: 10 feet times 400 mm
RIGHT: Convert the 400mm to feet first, OR convert the 10 feet to mm first. Then multiply.

Part 4: Practice Translation

The Scenario:
A plumber needs to install a pipe run of 12 meters. The pipe costs $4.50 per foot. Calculate the total cost, adding 13% tax.

Step 1: Translate the Units (Metric to Imperial)
We have meters, but the price is per foot. We must convert.

12 meters times 3.28 feet/meter = 39.36 feet.

Step 2: Translate "Per" (Multiplication)
39.36 times $4.50 = $177.12 (Subtotal).

Step 3: Translate "Tax" (The 1.X Multiplier)
177.12 times 1.13 = $200.14 (Total).

Final Answer: $200.14

APPLIED TRADES SCIENCE

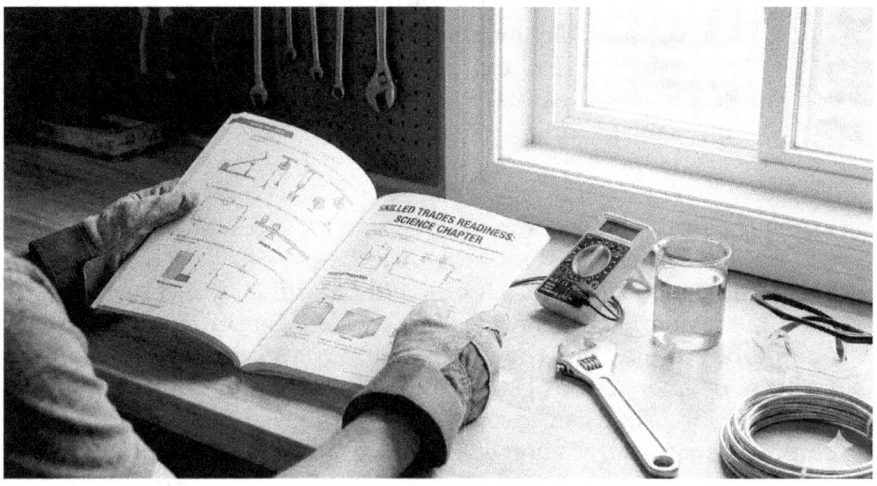

The Science Problems section of the Skilled Trades Readiness Test (STRT) measures your ability to understand and apply basic scientific concepts commonly used in the skilled trades. This section doesn't test advanced theory — instead, it focuses on practical, applied science that relates directly to real-world work environments such as construction, automotive, electrical, plumbing, and industrial trades.

You'll be asked to read short passages, interpret diagrams, and solve problems that involve physics, chemistry, and general science principles. Questions assess your ability to reason through cause-and-effect situations, apply formulas, and make logical predictions based on evidence or data.

.Typical topics include:

- **Forces and Motion:** Understanding how weight, friction, and pressure affect machines and tools.
- **Energy and Work:** Applying concepts of mechanical advantage, levers, and pulleys.
- **Electricity and Magnetism:** Basic current flow, voltage, and safety concepts relevant to trades work.
- **Heat and Temperature:** Understanding expansion, heat transfer, and insulation.
- **Matter and Materials:** Basic chemistry of metals, corrosion, and chemical reactions.
- **Scientific Measurement:** Reading gauges, scales, and interpreting simple graphs or tables.

The questions below are not the same as you will find on the Skilled Trades Test - that would be too easy! And nobody knows what the questions will be and they change all the time. Mostly the changes consist of substituting new questions for old, but the changes also can be new question formats or styles, changes to the number of questions in each section, changes to the time limits for each section and combing sections. Below are general Science questions that cover the same areas as the Skilled Trades Test. So, while the format and exact wording of the questions may differ slightly, and changes from year to year, if you can answer the questions below, you will have no problem with the natural science section of the Test.

Self Assessment

The purpose of the self-assessment is:

- Identify your strengths and weaknesses.
- Develop your personalized study plan (see Chapter 1)
- Get accustomed to the format

- Extra practice – the self-assessment is a 3rd test!
- Provide a baseline score for preparing your study schedule.

Since this is a self-assessment, and depending on how confident you are with Natural Science, timing yourself is optional. Once complete, use the table below to assess you understanding of the content, and prepare your study schedule described in chapter 1.

80% - 100%	Excellent – you have mastered the content
60 – 79%	Good. You have a working knowledge. Even though you can just pass this section, you may want to review the Tutorials and do some extra practice to see if you can improve your mark.
40% - 59%	Below Average. You do not understand the problems. Review the tutorials, and retake this quiz again in a few days, before proceeding to the rest of the practice test questions.
Less than 40%	Poor. You have a very limited understanding of the problems. Please review the Tutorials, and retake this quiz again in a few days, before proceeding to the rest of the study guide.

Science Self Assessment

	A	B	C	D
1	○	○	○	○
2	○	○	○	○
3	○	○	○	○
4	○	○	○	○
5	○	○	○	○
6	○	○	○	○
7	○	○	○	○
8	○	○	○	○
9	○	○	○	○
10	○	○	○	○
11	○	○	○	○
12	○	○	○	○
13	○	○	○	○
14	○	○	○	○
15	○	○	○	○

1. A hybrid car uses a battery-powered motor during low-speed driving and switches to a gasoline engine at higher speeds.

What is the main advantage of this design?

    a. It eliminates the need for refueling

    b. It reduces overall fuel consumption and emissions

    c. It increases the car's top speed

    d. It uses less electrical energy to charge the battery

2. A roller coaster car starts from rest at the top of a hill and rolls down without friction.

Which statement best describes the energy conversion as it moves down the hill?

    a. Kinetic energy is converted into potential energy

    b. Potential energy is converted into kinetic energy

    c. Mechanical energy is converted into chemical energy

    d. Thermal energy is converted into electrical energy

3. Farmers use cover crops (like clover or rye) during the off-season instead of leaving fields bare.

Which of the following is a major environmental benefit of this practice?

    a. It increases soil erosion during heavy rains

    b. It reduces soil fertility by absorbing nutrients

    c. It prevents nutrient loss and improves soil structure

    d. It increases pesticide runoff

4, A sealed carbonated drink is chilled in the refrigerator. When opened, fewer bubbles form compared to when the same drink is opened at room temperature.
What best explains this observation?

    a. Cold temperatures reduce gas solubility in liquids

    b. Cold temperatures increase gas solubility in liquids

    c. Warm air pushes gas out of the drink

    d. Cold liquids evaporate more quickly

5. What are considered to be the four fundamental forces of nature?

    a. Gravity, electromagnetic force, weak nuclear force, and strong nuclear force

    b. Gravity, electromagnetic force, negative nuclear force, and positive nuclear force

    c. Polarity, electromagnetic force, weak nuclear force, and strong nuclear force

    d. Gravity, chemical magnetic force, weak nuclear force, and strong nuclear force

6. Which of these statements about mechanical energy is/are true?

    a. Mechanical energy is the energy that is possessed by an object due to its motion or due to its position.

    b. Mechanical energy can be either kinetic energy (energy of motion) or potential energy (stored energy of position).

    c. Objects have mechanical energy if they are in motion

    d. All of the above.

7. Evaporation is:

a. A type of vaporization that occurs within the mass of a liquid

b. A type of vaporization that occurs from the surface of a liquid

c. A type of vaporization that occurs from the surface and within the mass of a liquid.

d. None of the above

8. During intense exercise, lactic acid builds up in muscle tissue. What is the most likely cause of this build-up?

a. The body is using oxygen more efficiently

b. The muscles are producing energy without enough oxygen

c. The heart rate decreases during exercise

d. The body's temperature drops too quickly

9. A student connects a light bulb to a battery using copper wires. If the wires are replaced with thinner wires of the same material, what will most likely happen?

a. The bulb will glow brighter

b. The bulb will glow dimmer

c. The bulb will not light at all

d. There will be no change

**10. Large bodies of water like oceans and lakes tend to keep nearby land areas cooler in summer and warmer in winter.
Which property of water best explains this effect?**

a. Water evaporates easily

b. Water heats up and cools down slowly

c. Water reflects sunlight

d. Water expands when it freezes

11. An engineer designs a home that uses geothermal heating. Which principle allows this system to provide heat in winter?

    a. Heat from the Earth's interior warms underground water or air

    b. Solar energy is stored in underground tanks

    c. Air pressure increases temperature below the surface

    d. Magnetic fields from the Earth create heat

12. When vinegar (acetic acid) reacts with baking soda (sodium bicarbonate), bubbles of carbon dioxide form. What type of reaction is this?

    a. Physical change

    b. Combustion reaction

    c. Acid–base reaction producing a gas

    d. Endothermic decomposition

13. A factory installs scrubbers in its smokestacks to remove sulfur dioxide before it is released into the atmosphere.

What environmental problem is this action most likely intended to reduce?

    a. Greenhouse gas accumulation

    b. Acid rain formation

    c. Ozone layer depletion

    d. Thermal pollution in rivers

14. A student connects two identical light bulbs in parallel to a battery. Compared to connecting the same bulbs in series, how will the bulbs in parallel appear?

    a. Both bulbs will be dimmer

    b. Both bulbs will be brighter

    c. Only one bulb will light

    d. Neither bulb will light

15. If the Earth's axis were not tilted, what major change would most likely occur?

    a. Days would be shorter at the poles

    b. Ocean tides would be stronger

    c. There would be no seasonal changes

    d. The Moon would stop revolving

Answer Key

1. B
The electric motor is efficient at low speeds; switching between electric and gasoline power saves fuel and reduces emissions.

2. C
Fewer red blood cells mean less oxygen is carried to muscles and organs, leading to fatigue.

3. C
Cover crops reduce erosion and nutrient loss, adding organic matter that improves soil quality.

4. B
Gas is more soluble in cold liquids, so less carbon dioxide escapes when opened cold.

5. A
The four fundamental forces of nature are, gravity, electromagnetic force, weak nuclear force, and strong nuclear force.

Note: Electromagnetic force is more commonly known as electricity.

6. D
All the statements are true.

    a. Mechanical energy is the energy that is possessed by an object due to its motion or due to its position.

    b. Mechanical energy can be either kinetic energy (energy of motion) or potential energy (stored energy of position).

    c. Objects have mechanical energy if they are in motion

7. B
Evaporation is a type of vaporization of a liquid that only occurs on the surface of a liquid. The other type of vaporization is boiling, which, instead, occurs within the entire mass of the liquid.

8. B
When oxygen is limited, muscles switch to anaerobic respiration, producing lactic acid as a byproduct.

9. B
Thinner wires have more resistance, reducing current flow, so the bulb glows dimmer.

10. B
Water has a high specific heat capacity — it absorbs and releases heat slowly, moderating nearby temperatures.

11. A
Geothermal systems draw on constant heat stored underground, transferring it to the home in winter.

12. C
Vinegar (acid) reacts with baking soda (base) to form carbon dioxide gas, water, and a salt — a classic acid–base reaction.

13. B
Sulfur dioxide combines with water vapor to form sulfuric acid, contributing to acid rain. Scrubbers remove SO_2 to reduce this effect.

14. B
In a parallel circuit, each bulb receives the full battery voltage, so both shine brighter than when connected in series

15. C
Earth's seasons are caused by the tilt of its axis. Without the tilt, there would be no seasonal temperature variation.

Basic Physics

Kinetic and Mechanical Energy

The kinetic energy of an object is the energy it possesses due to its motion.

>Kinetic energy is the work needed to accelerate a body of a given mass from rest to a stated velocity. Like all forms of energy, kinetic energy is measured in joules. Kinetic energy is imparted to an object when an energy source is tapped to accelerate it. It also happens when one object with kinetic energy slams into another object and kinetic energy from the first object is transferred to the second.

>However it happens, imparting kinetic energy to an object causes it to accelerate. Movement, therefore, is nothing more than an indication of the amount of kinetic energy an object has. An object will hold onto its kinetic energy until it is able to transfer it to something else, which allows it to slow down again.

While an object has the same level of kinetic energy, it will move at a consistent velocity forever. This is Newton's first law of motion.

The transfer of kinetic energy from one object to another can occur in many ways.

>The transfer of kinetic energy can be as simple and mundane as a baseball flying through the air—interacting with all the various molecules of oxygen, carbon dioxide, nitrogen and all the other gasses that make up our atmosphere, and transferring its kinetic energy to them—speeding them up and slowing itself down in the process. Or it can be as chaotic as a speeding truck losing control on an icy road and slamming into a wall.

Different types of interactions between objects appear to be different but are in fact the same.

>The interaction between the baseball and the air and between the truck and the wall are only superficially different. One appears more chaotic than the other only because of the differences in mass between a baseball and a truck and the differences in "negative energy" possessed by free-floating air molecules compared to a solid wall. At its most basic, however, the same events are taking place in both examples. Molecules in the wall and the air scatter when the kinetic energy they receive causes them to move, and this produces heat and sound.

Kinetic energy can be calculated with the formula KE = ½mv² where m is the mass of the object in kilograms, and v is its velocity in meters/second.

Kinetic energy increases by the square of an objects velocity.

>One important aspect of kinetic energy that makes it so potentially destructive is that the kinetic energy relative to not increase on pace with its velocity, but rather, relative to the square of its velocity. If you double an object's velocity, you will quadruple the kinetic energy it possesses (2²=4). If you quadruple the velocity, you increase the kinetic energy by sixteen times (4²=16). This leads to relatively small masses possessing very high kinetic energy levels when they are accelerated to only nominally high speeds. This is one reason why modern kinetic energy weapons (such as firearms) are able to cause large amounts of damage while being extremely compact.

Mechanical Energy

Mechanical energy is the ability of an object to do work.

>When discussing energy it is important to take a moment to understand mechanical energy and how it relates to the objects it interacts with. Mechanical

energy is not a separate type of energy in the way that potential energy and kinetic energy differ.

Mechanical energy is the potential energy available to an object added to all the kinetic energy available to it, providing a total energy output.

For instance, in our description of potential energy there is the example of a pole-vaulter hanging in mid-air with her pole bent at a near right angle to the ground. The bend in the pole-vaulter's pole contains elastic potential energy, which will help her clear the bar. However, that is not the only source of energy the pole-vaulter is restricted to. For anyone who has ever seen a track and field competition, you know that pole-vaulters take long, running starts before planting their poles in the ground. This imparts kinetic energy to the runners body, and it is that kinetic energy plus the pole's elastic potential energy that are added together in mid-air to impart the total mechanical energy that drives the pole-vaulter high into the air and over the bar.

Potential Energy

There are two main types of potential energy: gravitational potential energy and elastic potential energy.

Potential energy is the potential an object has to act on other objects. As gravitational potential energy, the object is raised off the ground and is waiting for the force of gravity pulling at $9.8 m/s^2$, to grab hold of it and pull it towards the Earth.

This type of energy is very common in everyday life. It describes everything from a book falling off its shelf to a child tripping on a crack in the sidewalk. Because gravitational potential energy is so common, the equation describing it PEgrav = mass * g * height should not be hard to figure out since it contains only easily observable features of matter: an object's mass, the force of gravity (g), and the object's height off the ground when it started falling.

Note that the height does not have to be measured from the ground. Any point can be chosen—such as a table top or even a point in mid-air—if you are only concerned with the energy an object would have if it fell from the point it was currently at to the point you have chosen.

Gravitational Potential Energy Example

If we take the example of a 1kg weight positioned at a height of 1 meter above the surface of Earth (where the gravity is $9.8 m/s^2$—try this on Mars and you will get a different result), we end with the equation PEgrav = 1 * 9.8 * 1, which equals 9.8 joules of gravitational potential energy. A 1g weight positioned at the same height would be PEgrav = .001 * 9.8 * 1 or .0098J of potential energy, while a 1kg weight positioned a kilometer up would equal PEgrav = 1 * 9.8 * 1000 or 9800J of potential energy.

From this equation you may have picked up on the fact that the height an object is raised, is directly proportional to the amount of gravitational potential energy it has. Take a 1kg object and raise it to 5m, and you get 49J of potential energy. Double that to 10m, and you get 98J. Triple it to 15m and you will get 147J—three times the original 49J.

Elastic Potential Energy

Elastic potential energy occurs when an object is stretched or compressed out of its normal "resting" shape. The quantity of energy that will be released when it finally returns to rest is the quantity of elastic potential energy it has while stretched or compressed.

A common example of elastic potential energy is when an archer draws back the string of his bow. The farther back the bowstring is pulled, the more it will stretch. The more it stretches the more potential energy it will have waiting to send into the arrow.

Elastic potential energy of an object can be determined using Hooke's law of elasticity. Hooke's law states that $F = -kx$ where F is the force the material will exert as it returns to its resting state measured in Newtons, x is amount of displacement the material undergoes measured in meters, and k is the spring constant and is measured in Newtons/meter.

To determine the potential energy of an elastic or springy material you use the equation $PE = 1/2\ kx^2$. According to this equation, an object such as a spring with a spring constant of 5N/m that is stretched 3 meters past its resting point would have a potential energy of 22.5J. That is, $½ * 5 * 3^2 = 2.5 * 9 = 22.5J$. Remember that elastic potential energy affects much more than just what you would consider elastic or springy material such as rubber bands, bungee cords and springs. There is elastic potential energy in a pole-vaulter's pole at the point where she is in the air and hanging onto a pole that is bent nearly sideways. In the next instant, her forward momentum will be boosted by the conversion of her pole's potential energy into kinetic energy, pushing her over the bar. Similarly, when a hockey player shoots the puck, he drags his stick along the ice as it moves forward, bending the shaft backwards slightly. This adds extra force to the puck as the stick snaps forward back into its normal resting position.

Energy: Work and Power

In the simplest terms, energy is the ability to do work.

Energy allows objects and people to effect the physical world and displace (or move) other objects or people.

Work in the physics sense is a very specific concept.

Measured in joules, defined as being 1 Newton of force that displaces something by 1 meter. (J = Nm) As the mass of the object being displaced varies, the quantity of work in joules required to move it a meter will vary too.

To determine the quantity of work being done, you can use the equation
W = F * d * cosΘ.

This defines work as the force applied, multiplied by the distance the object was displaced, multiplied by the cosine of Θ (Theta).

The force is measured in Newtons. Distance is measured in meters. The tricky part of this equation is determining the cosine of Θ. Θ represents the difference in angle between the vector (or direction) the force is acting in and the vector the displacement is occurring. That means that there are really only three possible values for Θ.

If the force is pushing or pulling in one direction, and the object being displaced is moving in that same direction, then there is no difference in angle between the vectors and Θ=0°. This is the sort of force you get when a child pulls her sled across a snowy field. The direction the child is pulling and the direction the sled is traveling are the same. Since cos0 = 1 the quantity of work is determined simply by multiplying the force and the displacement.

Note that the angle of the vectors is determined by their relationship, and not to an ideal flat surface. That is, if the child is pulling her sled up a steep hill rather than across a field, the angle of Θ is still going to be 0° since the force she exerts on the sled and the sled itself are still traveling in the same direction.

The second possibility is when the force vector acts in the opposite direction of the object's displacement. This gives what is called "negative work" because the energy is working to hinder the object from moving rather than to help it. In this instance Θ=180° since the vector in which the force is acting and the vector in which the object is moving are opposite. This force is most commonly observed when dealing with friction. It is the reason that hockey pucks and soccer balls will not travel forever; the force of friction exerted by the ice and by the grass is acting in the opposite direction.

The final difference in vectors is when the force being exerted on an object is at a right angle to its displacement. Here, $\Theta=90°$. You can picture this as a waitress carrying a tray of drinks over to your table, and it provides for some odd conclusions. Since the force we are talking about is the force the waitress is using to hold the tray vertically, but the displacement vector of the tray is horizontally across the room, we find that the force the waitress exerts no work at all. It is not responsible for moving the tray horizontally towards your table.

This is represented mathematically with the fact that the cos90 = 0, meaning that the original equation W = F * d * cosΘ would be W = F * d * 0. Without adding any additional information, it is obvious that work is going to equal zero joules.

A different way to imagine this is to think of cargo in the back of a truck.

It took work to load the cargo up onto the truck from the ground (the force vector and the displacement vector were both pointing in the same direction), but once the cargo was loaded, no additional work was required to keep it there. The truck could drive from one end of the country to the other, but zero joules of work would be exerted keeping the cargo in place in the back of the truck.

When you add a unit of time to your calculations of work, you get a new classification: power.

Power is the rate at which work is done. The equation that measures power, is power = work/time. In this equation work is measured in joules, time is measured in seconds and power is measured in watts. Since, as we noted above, one joule is the same as one Newton multiplied by one meter, this equation can also be written as power=(force*displacement)/time where force is measured in Newtons and displacement is measured in meters. However, this opens further possibilities. Since the math does not care if we first multiply force with displacement before dividing the whole thing by time, or we divide displacement by time, and then multiply the answer by force, we find the equation can also be written as power = force(displacement/time).

Given that displacement is measured in meters and the time in seconds, what we are really saying here is that power equals the amount of force applied to an object multiplied by that object's velocity (m/s).

Thus we get two equations describing power: power = work/time and power=force*velocity.

By definition, power has an inverse relationship with time; the less time that it takes for the work to be done, the more power is being applied. Power also has a direct relationship with force and velocity. Increase either the quantity of force being applied to an object, or the speed at which it is traveling, and you have increased the power.

Defining Force and Newton's Three Laws

In physics force is the term given to anything that has the power to act on an object, causing its displacement in one direction or another.

to identify accurately, and therefore it took thousands of years to identify accurately and describe them. It was not until the 17th century that Isaac Newton described the basic physical forces and show how they acted on matter.

Force is measured using the unit Newton (N). One Newton can be defined with the formula $1N = 1kg(1m/s^2)$. In other words, if you accelerate a kilogram of matter by one meter per second per second, you have exerted one Newton of force on it.

Newton developed three laws to explain the interactions of matter he observed. The first is often known as the "Law of Inertia."

It states that an object at rest will stay at rest, and an object in motion will stay in motion, unless a force acts on it to change its state. This means that if you fire a spaceship out into the vacuum of space, and keep it clear from planets and stars that will apply force to it, the ship will keep going at the same speed forever.

This tendency to stay moving or stay at rest is known as inertia. Inertia is directly related to an object's mass; the more mass an object has, the more inertia it will have, and the more difficult to speed it up or slow it down. This is implied by the equation defining one Newton of force, but it is also obvious in everyday life. You have to exert more force to push a box of books across the floor than you would to push a box of clothes the same size. The box of books has more mass, so it has more inertia. Similarly, a baseball player can easily catch and stop a baseball thrown at over 100km/hr. If you were to ask that same player to stop a truck traveling at 100km/hr, you would get much less pleasant results.

One important thing to remember about force is that it is a vector quantity, meaning that it points in a specific direction.

Set a one kilogram object down on a table and you will have the force of gravity pulling it down at one Newton, and the force of all the atoms in the table pushing it up at one Newton. This is said to be a state of equilibrium, and it causes no change to the object's velocity. However, if the table had been poorly built and was only capable of pushing up at .75 Newtons, the object would pull through, snapping the table at its weakest points, and fall until it found something that was capable of applying the needed force to hold it up against gravity.

As such, an object can only be at rest if it has no forces acting on it, or if it has equal and opposite forces acting on it keeping it at equilibrium. If an unopposed force acts on an object, it will move.

Newton's second law deals with what happens when you have the sort of unbalanced forces that we just described.

It explains the movement of objects through the equation $F=ma$, where F is the force in Newtons, m is the object's mass in kilograms, and a is the object's acceleration in meters per second per second (m/s2). Just like with Newton's first law, this equation shows that mass is very important when it comes to using a force to move objects. The larger the mass, the more force you will need to accelerate or decelerate it to the same velocity.

Newton's third law states simply that for every action there is an equal and opposite reaction.

This means that if I pound my hand down on my desk right now, my desk will also be hitting up at my hand with the exact same force. This may sound strange, but it is the reason that pounding your hand on your desk can damage your desk and hurt your hand at the same time. It is also the reason that baseball bats can snap while imparting force onto the ball, and why a moving car hitting stationary wall will damage both.

Force: Friction

Friction is the force that resists the motion of objects relative to other objects.

When two surfaces move relative to each other, the force of friction is what slows them down. Friction applies to all matter, whether it is a book sliding down a slanting shelf, a soccer ball rolling on the ground or a baseball flying though the air. Friction is a constant opposing force that keeps things from traveling forever.

Several laws describe how friction works.

Amontons' first law of friction says that, "The force of friction is directly proportional to the applied load." His second law of friction says that, "The force of friction is independent of the apparent area of contact." Similarly, Coulomb's law of friction states that, "Kinetic friction is independent of the sliding velocity."

The two main types of Friction are static friction and kinetic friction.

Static friction is what you get when one stationary object is stacked on top of another stationary object, such as a book resting on a table. The static friction between the book and the table determines how much sticking power there is between them, and at what angle you would have to tilt the table before the force of gravity overpowers the force of friction and starts the book sliding.

To calculate the maximum amount of static friction possible before the book starts sliding, you use the formula $f_s = \mu_s F_n$ where f_s is the total amount of static friction, μ_s (pronounced "mu") is the coefficient of static friction and F_n is the "normal force," the force being exerted perpendicularly through the surface into the object resting on it, keeping the object from breaking through the surface.

Another way to examine static friction is to calculate the angle the table will have to reach before the book will start sliding.

This is also known as the angle of repose, and it can be calculated using the formula $\tan\theta = \mu s$ where θ (pronounced "theta") is the angle of repose, and μs is the coefficient of static friction.

Aside from determining the angles that books will slide off tables, calculating static friction allows tire manufacturers to determine how "grippy" their treads are. If there were no friction, the wheel would not be a functional tool because it would not push itself against the road while moving. The higher the coefficient of friction between the tire and the road, the more grip the tire has.

Kinetic friction is like the inverse of static friction.

It is the force that causes moving objects to slow down. Kinetic friction applies to two surfaces moving relative to each other such as the bottom of a snowboard and the snowy ground. It can be calculated using the same basic formula used to calculate static friction: $fk = \mu k F n$ with the only differences being the sub-k marks replacing the sub-s marks of the previous equation, signifying kinetic friction.

As kinetic friction slows an object, the object's kinetic energy is transformed into heat.

Fundamental Forces: Electromagnetism

Electromagnetism is one of the four fundamental forces. It is far more common than gravity, but only if you know where to look.

Electromagnetism is responsible for nearly all interactions in which gravity plays no part. It is what holds negatively charged electrons in orbit around the positively charged protons in the nucleus of an atom. It is also the force that joins atoms to create molecules.

It is also electromagnetism that is responsible for the fact that matter—which is made up of atoms and at the subatomic level is mostly empty space—feels solid.

When you sit down in your chair, it is the electromagnetic attraction between the chair's atoms and between your body's atoms that keep you from falling through the chair and, conversely, that keep the chair from passing through you.

Electromagnetic force acts through a field.

This type of field can occur as a result of positively or negatively charged atoms (ions), atoms which have either more or fewer electrons than protons causing their overall charge to be unbalanced. Magnetic fields can also be created by applying electric current to conductive material (such as wire) with a conductive core (such as a nail).

Electric current is nothing more than a steady flow of electrons, and by turning on the current you send electrons through the core.

This aligns all the atoms in the metal so that they are parallel, and this creates a magnetic field. When you turn the electric current off, the electrons stop flowing, and the atoms, no longer forced by the current to line up, cease to be magnetic.

All electromagnetic fields have a positive and a negative pole.

Even the Earth's magnetic field, which is caused by the convective forces in the planet's core, sends electrons out of its negative pole (in the geographic North Pole) and reaccepts them at its positive pole (in the geographic South Pole in Antarctica). The Earth's magnetic field, like all magnetic fields, is able to effect charged particles.

Magnetic fields move in one direction around a magnet.

This direction is always the same relative to the flow of current from negative to positive poles, and it is easy to test the direction of the field using the "right hand rule." Close your fist and make a "thumbs up" sign with your right hand. The positive pole is represented by the tip of your thumb, the negative by the other end of your hand, and the direction of the magnetic field by where your closed fingers are. Thus, if you point your thumb at yourself, your magnet has current coming out its negative pole pointed towards you and looping back around to the positive pole pointed away from you, and the field is pointed counter-clockwise, which here is to your left.

The effects of a magnetic field do not go on forever but follow the inverse square law.

The farther you move from a magnetic field, the less its force will effect you. By moving x times away from a magnetic field, you feel $1/x2$ times less magnetism.

Closely related to the electromagnetic field is electromagnetic radiation.

This radiation can take many forms, the most familiar are light, radio waves that carry radio and broadcast television, microwaves that cook our food, x-rays that can image the insides or our bodies, and gamma rays that come down from space and would have killed us all long ago if it were not for the Earth's magnetic field interacting with them.

Electromagnetic radiation is created, according to James Clerk Maxwell, by the oscillations of electromagnetic fields, which create electromagnetic waves.

The wave's frequency (or how energetic it is) determines what part of the electromagnetic spectrum it occupies—whether it is a gamma ray, a blue light or a radio signal. Electromagnetic radiation is the same thing as light, with what we are used to as visible light being a range of specific frequencies within the electromagnetic spectrum, so all electromagnetic

radiation moves at the speed of light.

At the quantum level, the electromagnetic force has a transfer particle moving between charged atoms, attracting and repelling them. The electromagnetic transfer particle is the photon.

Fundamental Forces: Gravity

Gravity may be the most commonly, consciously experienced force.

> We can see its effects everyday when books fall off shelves, when stray baseballs arc downwards and crash through windows and when Australians time and again fail to fall off the bottom of the world and out into space. Gravity is also largely responsible for the structure of the universe. Without it, stars would not ignite and begin fusion reactions, planets would not condense out of dust and metal and most matter would have no attraction to other matter in any way. Without gravity, life would not exist.

It may seem strange to learn that gravity is the weakest of all forces given that it holds the entire galaxy together.

> Still, even with the gravitational mass of the entire planet pulling on an object such as a ball—causing it to sit motionless on the floor rather than float aimlessly off into space—a toddler could easily pick it up and run off with it, and there would be nothing the planet could do about it. Match that with the

force an electromagnet exerts on metal; there is no comparison.

The idea of gravity as a force was first formulated by Isaac Newton in the late 17th century.

Newton's ideas were further elaborated on in the early 20th century by Albert Einstein, who described gravity as the effect of mass warping the fabric of space-time. This process is often portrayed as a large ball creating a divot in a flat sheet of space-time. The divot curves space-time and can catch objects that would otherwise be traveling in straight lines and redirect or even capture them.

On Earth gravity pulls objects towards the center of the planet at 9.8 m/s^2.

The squared rate of time shows that gravity is by its nature a force causing acceleration. Every second, the force of gravity increases the speed of an object by an additional 9.8 m/s, provided nothing able to resist the force gets in its way.

In Einstein's view of the universe, gravity moved in waves, which traveled through space at the speed of light.

As a result, he demonstrated that the force of gravity would take time to reach the object it was acting on. If, for instance, the sun were to vanish suddenly from the solar system, it would take eight minutes for the Earth to go flying off into space—the same amount of time it would take for us to stop seeing the sun's light.

Another way to view gravity is through a series of transfer particles that interact with matter and draw it closer together.

Transfer particles come into play in quantum mechanics, and they replace gravity waves as the method of spreading the force through the universe. (Actually, replace is not the right word, as quantum mechanics shows that particles and waves are really the same thing, simply looked at from different perspectives.) In quantum mechanics gravity's transfer particle is called a graviton, and it moves at the speed of light.

The farther you move from a gravitational mass, the less its force will affect you.

The drop in the gravitational force is governed by what is known as the inverse square law, which says the attraction of any object drops relative to the square of the distance you move from it. If you are floating over the surface of the planet and then move x times away from it, you will feel $1/x^2$ times less gravity. So if you move 10 times farther away from where you were, you will feel 1/100 the force gravity.

Speed, Acceleration and Force Problems

Acceleration

Acceleration is the rate velocity changes over time. A car starts from a zero speed in a straight line at increasing speed, it is accelerating in the direction of travel. If the car changes direction at the same speed, this is by definition acceleration, though not described as such; passengers in linear acceleration experience a force pushing them straight back, and a sideways force if the direction changes.

The formula for acceleration = A = $(V_f - V_0)/t$ and is measured in meters per second^2.

Here is a typical question:

A car starts from standing top and in 10 seconds is traveling 20/meters per second. What is the acceleration?

    a. 0.5 m/sec²
    b. 1.5 m/sec²
    c. 1 m/sec²
    d. 2 m/sec²

The formula for acceleration = $A = (V_f - V_o)/t$
so $A = (20 \text{ m/sec} - 0 \text{ m/sec})/10 \text{ sec} = 2 \text{ m/sec}^2$

Speed

Speed is the rate of change of an objects position, or, speed = (total distance traveled)/(total time taken).

Here is a typical question:

A rocket travels 3000 meters in 5 seconds. How fast is it traveling?

    a. 100 m/sec
    b. 200 m/sec
    c. 500 m/sec
    d. 600 m/sec

Speed = (total distance traveled)/(total time taken)
3000/5 = 600 meters per second.

Force

An everyday definition of Force is the push or pull. The more scientific definition of Force is any influence that causes an object to change its movement or direction. Force is measured in Newtons, (usually N) named after Sir Isaac Newton, and his formulation of the Second Law of motion, $F = ma$, where F = force, m = mass and a = acceleration.

$1\text{ N} = 1 \text{ kg m/s}^2$.

Therefore,

Force = Mass times Acceleration Measured in Newtons.
Acceleration is the change in speed over time.
Speed is the change in position over time.

Here is a typical question:
How much force is needed to accelerate a car that weights 500 kg to 10 m/s^2?

    a. 20,000 N
    b. 30,000 N
    c. 40,000 N
    d. 50,000 N

Force = Mass times Acceleration Measured in Newtons.
F = 500 X 10 = 50,000 N

Momentum

Momentum is the sum of the mass of an object and its velocity. This means that momentum measures the force produced by an object's mass and velocity.

For example, a very heavy object moving fast has a large momentum—it takes a large and prolonged force to get a very heavy object up to this speed, and it takes a large and prolonged force to bring it to a stop afterwards. If the object were lighter, or moving more slowly, then it would have less momentum, and it would be easier (i.e. require less force) to bring it to a stop.

The formula for calculating momentum is = Momentum = mass x velocity
Or
P = MV
Where P = momentum, V = velocity and M = mass

Based on the above definition, clearly the momentum of a car and a bicycle both traveling at 20 m/s will not be the same, because although the velocity of the two objects are the same, their mass is different. The car would have greater momentum, due to its larger mass.

Note:

The SI unit for velocity = m/s
SI unit for Mass = kg
So therefore momentum = kg x m/s and the SI unit for momentum is kg x m/s

Momentum must always have a direction and so the final answer must reflect the direction of the momentum or velocity.

Here is a typical question:

What is the momentum of a log weighing 700 kg that is rolling down a hill at 4.6 m/s?

    a. 3220 kg x m/s down the hill
    b. 3320 kg x m/s
    c. 3320 down hill
    d. 3320 M

Answer: A

P = MV
P = 700 X 4.6
P = 3220 kg x m/s down the hill.

Understanding Mechanical Systems

Section Overview: Mechanical Comprehension This section includes two parts: Mechanical Tutorials and a Self-Assessment.

The Tutorials are designed to review the fundamental principles of mechanics and engineering. Please note that these tutorials are not intended to replace a full physics course; they assume a basic familiarity with how mechanical systems work. If you find the core concepts difficult to grasp, we recommend seeking out additional introductory resources before proceeding.

The Self-Assessment includes questions designed to assess your understanding of these principles. While not identical to the official exam questions, they cover the exact same physical laws and mechanical concepts.

Key Subject Areas: The questions focus on the following core Engineering and Mechanical concepts:

Simple Machines: Levers, Pulleys, and Belts.

Motion & Force: Gears, Springs, and Acceleration.

Foundational Knowledge: Basic Physics principles.

Mechanical Comprehension

	A	B	C	D
1	○	○	○	○
2	○	○	○	○
3	○	○	○	○
4	○	○	○	○
5	○	○	○	○
6	○	○	○	○
7	○	○	○	○
8	○	○	○	○
9	○	○	○	○
10	○	○	○	○
11	○	○	○	○
12	○	○	○	○
13	○	○	○	○
14	○	○	○	○
15	○	○	○	○
16	○	○	○	○
17	○	○	○	○
18	○	○	○	○
19	○	○	○	○
20	○	○	○	○

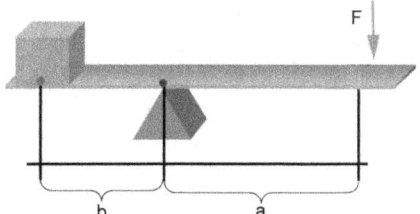

1. Consider the illustration above and the corresponding data:

Weight = W = 200 pounds
Distance from fulcrum to Weight = b = 10 feet
Distance from fulcrum to point where force is applied = a = 20 feet
How much force (F) must be applied to lift the weight?

    a. 80
    b. 100
    c. 150
    d. 200

2. A force of 20 kg. is applied to two springs in series, which compresses the springs 6 inches. If the same force is applied to springs in parallel, how far will the springs compress?

    a. 6 inches
    b. 3 inches
    c. 2 inches
    d. 1 inch

3. You are asked to determine the gear ratio of a vehicle. You open the differential and observe the ring gear the and pinion gear. The ring gear has 40 teeth and the pinion gear has 8, What is the gear ratio of the vehicle?

    a. 4:1
    b. 5:1
    c. 8:2
    d. 8:0

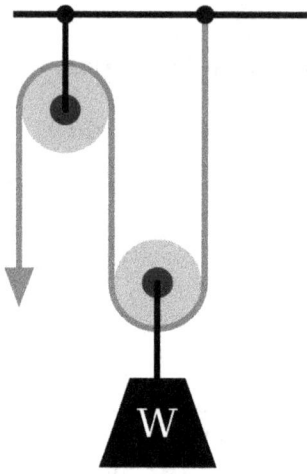

4. Consider the pulley arrangement above. If the weight, W, is 50 pounds, how much force is required to lift it?

    a. 10 pounds
    b. 20 pounds
    c. 25 pounds
    d. 50 pounds

5. Consider a gear train with 3 gears, from left to right, A with 20 teeth, gear B with 60 teeth, and gear C with 10 teeth. Gear A turns clockwise at 60 rpm. What direction and speed in rpm does Gear C turn?

    a. 120 rpm, clockwise

    b. 100 rpm clockwise

    c. 120 rpm counter clockwise

    d. 140 rpm counter clockwise

6. If a 100-pound object is sitting on a 10-square-inch plate, what is the PSI?

    a. 5

    b. 10

    c. 15

    d. 20

7. What is mechanical advantage?

    a. The ratio of energy input to energy output, typically where the input is less than the output.

    b. The ratio of energy input to energy output, typically where the input is greater than the output.

    c. The ratio of energy resistance to energy output, typically where the resistance is less than the output.

    d. None of the above

8. What is the ratio of mechanical advantage of a simple pulley?

    a. 2:1

    b. 1:1

    c. 3:1

    d. 1:2

9. Consider moving an object with a lever and a fulcrum. What is the relationship between the distance from the fulcrum and the speed the object will move?

    a. The farther away from the fulcrum, the faster the object will move.

    b. The closer to the fulcrum, the faster an object will move.

    c. An object will move the fastest when directly above the fulcrum.

    d. None of the above.

10. Which of the following are examples of a wedge?

    a. Corkscrew

    b. Scissors

    c. Wheelbarrow

    d. Pulley

11. Which of the following illustrates the principal of the lever?

    a. The greater the distance over which the force is applied, the greater the force required (to lift the load).

    b. The greater the distance over which the force is applied, the smaller the force required (to lift the load).

    c. The smaller the distance over which the force is applied, the smaller the force required (to lift the load).

    d. None of the above

12. Consider two gears on separate shafts that mesh. The input gear has 30 teeth and turns at 100 rpm. If the output gear has 40 teeth, how fast is the output gear turning?

    a. 300 rpm

    b. 250 rpm

    c. 75 rpm

    d. 100 rpm

13. Consider two gears on separate shafts that mesh. The input gear has 100 teeth and turns at 50 rpm. If the output gear has 20 teeth, how fast is the output gear turning?

    a. 300 rpm
    b. 250 rpm
    c. 200 rpm
    d. 100 rpm

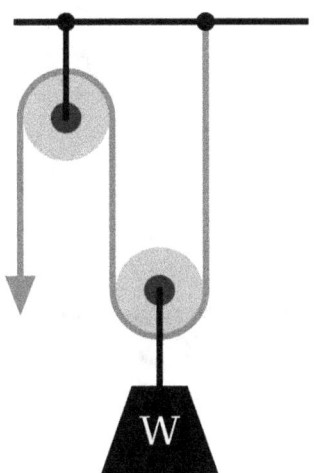

14. Consider the pulley arrangement above. If the weight is 100 pounds, how much force is required to lift it?

    a. 20 pounds
    b. 33 pounds
    c. 50 pounds
    d. 75 pounds

15. Tension of 40 kg. is applied to two springs in parallel, which expands the springs 8 inches. If the same force is applied to springs in series, how far will the springs expand?

   a. 2 inches
   b. 4 inches
   c. 8 inches
   d. 16 inches

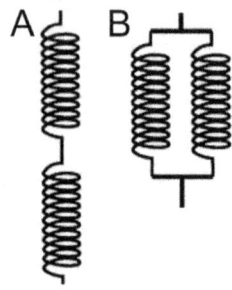

16. Consider the diagram above and select the correct labels from the options below.

   a. A - series, B - parallel
   b. A - parallel, B - series
   c. Series and parallel do not apply to springs
   d. None of the above

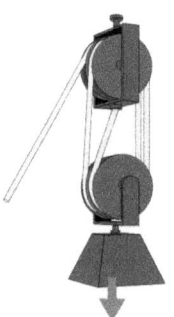

17. Consider the pulley arrangement above. If the weight is 200 pounds, how much force must be exerted downward on the rope?

   a. 200 pounds
   b. 100 pounds
   c. 50 pounds
   d. 25 pounds

18. Up-and-down or back-and-forth motion is called:

   a. Rotary motion
   b. Reciprocating motion
   c. Agitation motion
   d. Harmonic motion

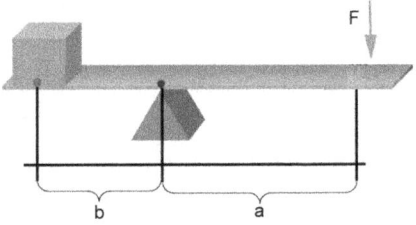

19. Consider the illustration above and the corresponding data:
Weight = W = 80 pounds
Distance from fulcrum to Weight = b = 10 feet
Distance from fulcrum to point where force is applied = a = 20 feet
How much force (F) must be applied to lift the weight?

   a. 80
   b. 40
   c. 20
   d. 10

20. The output torque of a 2 gear train is 1,000 newton-meters, and the gear ratio is 2:1. What is the input force?

    a. 200

    b. 400

    c. 500

    d. 1000

Answer Key

1. B
To solve for F, Weight X b (distance from fulcrum to weight) = Force X a (distance from fulcrum to point where force is applied)
200 X 10 = F X 20
2000/20 = F
F = 100

2. B
If the springs in series compress 6 inches, then the springs in parallel will compress half that amount, or 3 inches.

3. B
Opening the differential, the ring gear is the larger gear and the pinion the smaller. The gear differential is calculated by dividing the number of teeth on the pinion into the number of teeth on the ring gear. 40/8 = 5, or 5:1.

4. C
Since the weight is only attached to one pulley, the force required will be 50/2 = 25 pounds.

5. A
First calculate the speed of gear B. The gear ratio is 60:20 or 3:1. If gear A is turning at 60 rpm, then gear B will turn at 30/3 = 20 rpm.

Next calculate B and C. Gear C is smaller, so it will turn faster. The gear ratio is 60:10 or 6:1, and since gear B turns at 20 rpm, gear C will turn at 20 X 6 = 120 rpm.

Next calculate the direction. Gear A is turning clockwise, so Gear B is turning counter-clockwise, so gear C must be turning clockwise.

6. B
Calculate the PSI by taking the weight divided by the size of the object the weight is bearing on. 100/10 = 10 PSI.

7. A

Mechanical advantage is the ratio of energy input to energy output, typically where the input is less than the output. Mechanical advantage is a measure of the force amplification achieved by using a tool, mechanical device or machine system. Ideally, the device preserves the input power and simply trades off forces against movement to obtain a desired amplification in the output force. The model for this is the law of the lever. Machine components designed to manage forces and movement in this way are called mechanisms.

8. B

The ratio of mechanical advantage of a simple pulley is 1:1.

9. A

The farther away from the fulcrum, the faster the object will move.

10. B

Examples of wedges include the cutting edge of scissors, knives, screwdrivers, doorstops, nails axes and chisels.

11. B

The greater the distance over which the force is applied, the smaller the force required (to lift the load).

12. C

Call the input gear G^1 and the output gear G^2. Call the speed of G^1, S^1 and the number of teeth T^1. Similarly for G^2, we have S^2 and T^2.
Given data:
$S^1 = 100$
$T^1 = 30$
S^2 = unknown
$T^2 = 40$
We know that $S^1 \times T^1 = S^2 \times T^2$
So, $100 \times 30 = S^2 \times 40$
$S^2 = 3000/40 = 75$ rpm

13. B

Call the input gear G^1 and the output gear G^2. Call the speed of G^1, S^1 and the number of teeth T^1. Similarly for G^2, we have S^2 and T^2.

Given data
$S^1 - 50$
$T^1 = 100$
$S^2 = $ unknown
$T^2 = 20$
We know that $S^1 \times T^1 = S^2 \times T^2$

So, $50 \times 100 = S^2 \times 20$
$S^2 = 5000/20 = 250$ rpm

14. B
Notice the weight is attached to one end of the rope and to one pulley. The force required to lift a 100 pound weight with this arrangement is 100/3 = 33.

15. A
If the springs in parallel expand 10 inches, then the springs in series will expand twice that amount, or 20 inches.

16. A
The correct labels are, A - series, B - parallel

17. C
50 pounds of force much be exerted downward on the rope to lift the 200 pound weight. Since there are 4 pulleys, each will take 1/4 of the load. 200/4 = 50 pounds.

18. B
Up-and-down or back-and-forth motion is called reciprocal motion.

19. B
To solve for F, Weight X b (distance from fulcrum to weight) = Force X a (distance from fulcrum to point where force is applied)
$80 \times 10 = F \times 20$
$800/20 = F$
$F = 40$

20. C
If the output force is 1,000 newton-meters, and the gear ration is 2:1, the input force will be 1,000/2 = 500.

Overview of Simple Machines

1. Lever

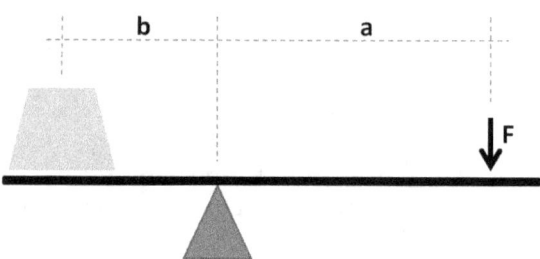

The lever is a movable bar that pivots on a fulcrum attached to a fixed point. The lever operates by applying forces at different distances from the fulcrum, or pivot.

Assuming the lever does not dissipate or store energy, the power into the lever must equal the power out of the lever. As the lever rotates around the fulcrum, points farther from this pivot move faster than points closer to the pivot. Therefore a force applied to a point farther from the pivot must be less than the force located at a point closer in, because power is the product of force and velocity.

This is the law of the lever, which was proven by Archimedes using geometric reasoning. It shows that if the distance a from the fulcrum to where the input force is applied (point A) is greater than the distance b from fulcrum to where the output force is applied (point B), then the lever amplifies the input force. On the other hand, if the distance a from the fulcrum to the input force is less than the distance b from the fulcrum to the output force, then the lever reduces the input force.

Here is a sample question:

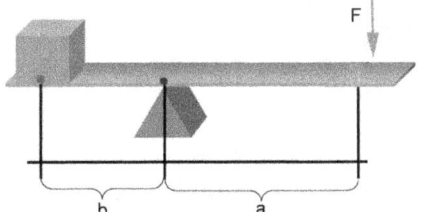

Consider the illustration above and the corresponding data:

Weight = W = 100 pounds
Distance from fulcrum to Weight = b = 2 feet
Distance from fulcrum to point where force is applied = a = 5 feet
How much force (F) must be applied to lift the weight?

a. 100
b. 40
c. 25
d. 10

Answer: B

Solution:

We know that the lever does not store energy, so the to solve for F, Weight X b (distance from fulcrum to weight) = Force X a (distance from fulcrum to point where force is applied)
100 X 2 = F X 5
200/5 = F
F = 40

2. Pulleys

A pulley is a wheel on an axle that is designed to support movement of a cable or belt along its circumference. Pulleys are used in a variety of ways to lift loads, apply forces, and to transmit power.

A pulley is also called a sheave or drum and may have a groove between two flanges around its circumference. The drive element of a pulley system can be a rope, cable, belt, or chain that runs over the pulley inside the groove.

A rope and pulley system, that is a block and tackle, is characterized by the use of a single continuous rope to transmit a tension force around one or more pulleys to lift or move a load—the rope may be a light line or a strong cable.

If the rope and pulley system does not dissipate or store energy, then its mechanical advantage is the number of parts of the rope that act on the load. This can be shown as follows.

Consider the set of pulleys that form the moving block and the parts of the rope that support this block. If there are p of these parts of the rope supporting the load W, then a force balance on the moving block shows that the tension in each of the parts of the rope must be W/p. This means the input force on the rope is T=W/p. Thus, the block and tackle reduces the input force by the factor p.

3. Wedge

A wedge is a triangular shaped round tool, a compound and portable inclined plane, and one of the six classical simple machines. It can be used to separate two objects or portions of an object, lift an object, or hold an object in place. It functions by converting a force applied to its blunt end into forces perpendicular (normal) to its inclined surfaces. The mechanical advantage of a wedge is given by the ratio of the length of its slope to its width. Although a short wedge with a wide angle may do a job faster, it requires more force than a long wedge with a narrow angle.

4. Screw

A screw is a mechanism that converts rotational motion to linear motion, and a torque (rotational force) to a linear force. It is one of the six classical simple machines. The most common form consists of a cylindrical shaft with helical grooves or ridges called threads around the outside. The screw passes through a hole in another object or medium, with threads on the inside of the hole that mesh with the screw's threads.

A screw can amplify force; a small rotational force (torque) on the shaft can exert a large axial force on a load. The smaller the pitch, the distance between the screw's threads, the greater the mechanical advantage, the ratio of output to input force. Screws are widely used in threaded fasteners to hold objects together, and in devices such as screw tops for containers, vises, screw jacks and screw presses.

5. Gears and Gear Trains

A gear train is formed by mounting gears on a frame so that the teeth of the gears engage. Gear teeth are designed to ensure the pitch circles of engaging gears roll on each other without slipping, this provides a smooth transmission of rotation from one gear to the next.

Here is a sample question:

Consider 3 meshed gears. Gear A has 20 teeth, Gear B has 60 teeth and Gear C has 10 teeth. Gear A revolves clockwise at 60 rpm. How fast does gear C turn and in what direction?

First, figure out the direction because that is easier. Gear A turn clockwise, which will turn gear B counter-clockwise. Now gear C, meshed with gear B will turn clockwise.

To calculate the speed of gear C, first calculate the speed of gear B.

To calculate the speed of gear B, first calculate the gear ration by,
No. of teeth of gear B / No. of teeth of gear A

60/20 = 3 (or gear ratio of 1:3 : Gear B : Gear A)

So gear B will turn 3 times for every complete turn of gear A. To calculate the speed of gear B, divide, 60/3 = 20 rpm.

This makes sense since gear B is three times the size of gear A (60 teeth to gear A's 20) so it turns much slower.

To calculate the speed of gear C, calculate the gear ration and then divide by the speed of gear B.

Notice that gear C is quite a bit smaller (10 teeth to gear B's 60 teeth), so we expect gear C will turn much faster.

First calculate the gear ratio: 60/10 = 6, or 6:1 : Gear C : Gear B.

Gear B is turning at 20 rpm - multiplying the speed is, 20 rpm X 6 = 120.

Gear C is turning at 120 rpm.

Spatial Visualization

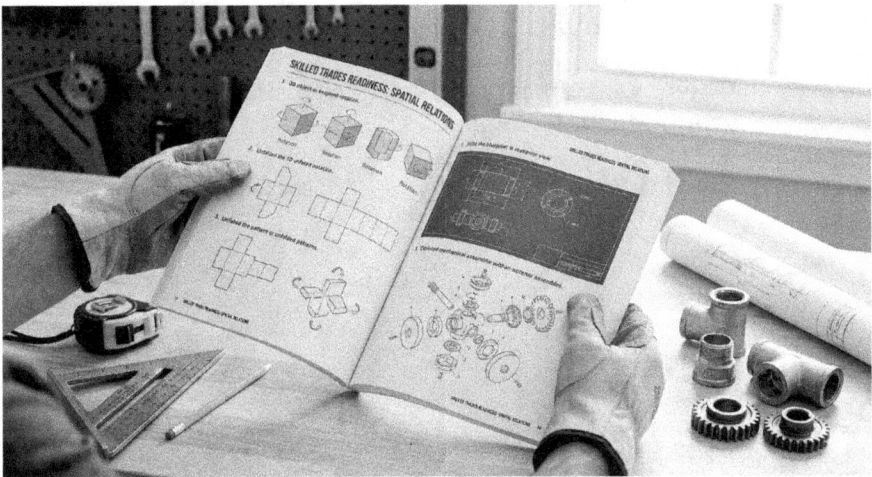

Section Overview: Spatial Visualization This section includes two parts: Spatial Reasoning Tutorials and a Self-Assessment.

The Tutorials are designed to review the strategies used to solve spatial problems, such as mental rotation and pattern folding. Please note that these tutorials are not a comprehensive geometry course; they assume a basic ability to visualize objects in three dimensions. If you find visualization difficult, we recommend using physical manipulatives (like folding paper boxes) to practice before proceeding.

The Self-Assessment includes questions designed to assess your ability to mentally manipulate shapes and objects. While not identical to the official exam questions, they require the exact same cognitive skills used on the Skilled Trades Test.

Key Subject Areas: The questions focus on your ability to visualize objects in 2D and 3D space. Common question types include:

Pattern Folding: Visualizing how a 2D flat pattern folds into a 3D object.

Mental Rotation: Identifying what an object looks like when rotated.

Object Matching: Identifying identical shapes from a group of similar objects.

Spatial Views: Matching a 3D object to its top, front, or side view.

Spatial Answer Sheet

	A	B	C	D
1	○	○	○	○
2	○	○	○	○
3	○	○	○	○
4	○	○	○	○
5	○	○	○	○
6	○	○	○	○
7	○	○	○	○
8	○	○	○	○
9	○	○	○	○
10	○	○	○	○
11	○	○	○	○
12	○	○	○	○
13	○	○	○	○
14	○	○	○	○
15	○	○	○	○
16	○	○	○	○
17	○	○	○	○
18	○	○	○	○
19	○	○	○	○
20	○	○	○	○

1. When the two longest sides touch what will the shape be?

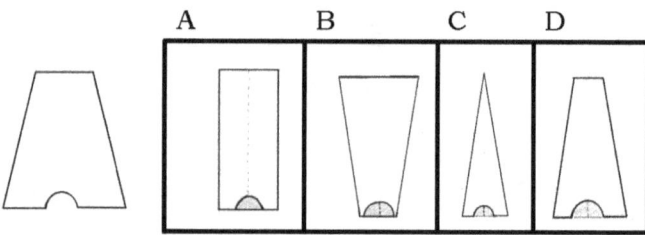

2. When folded, what pattern is possible?

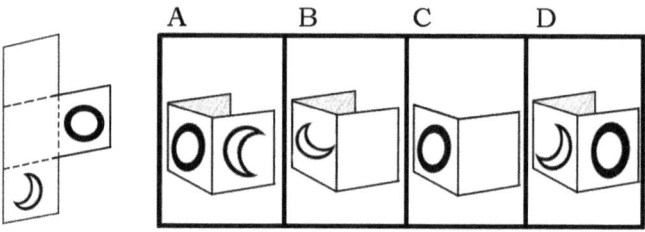

3. When folded into a loop, what will the strip of paper look like?

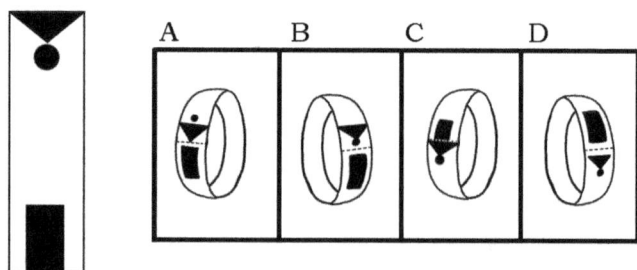

4. Which of the choices is the same pattern at a different angle?

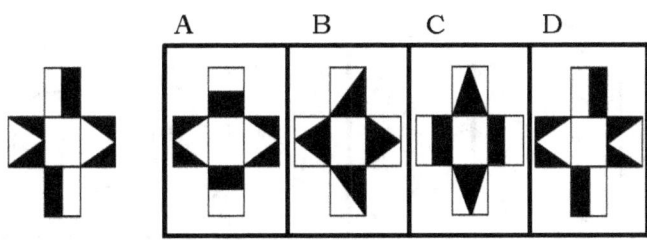

5. When put together, what 3-dimensional shape will you get?

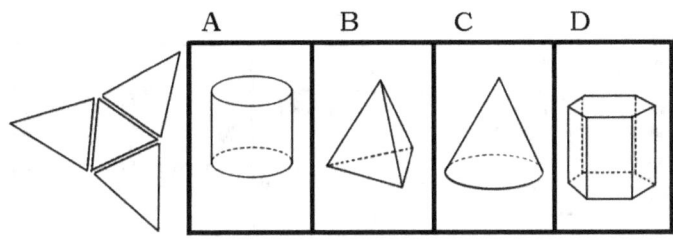

6. When folded, what pattern is possible?

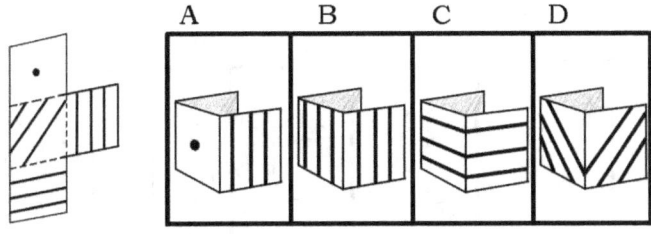

7. When folded into a loop, what will the strip of paper look like?

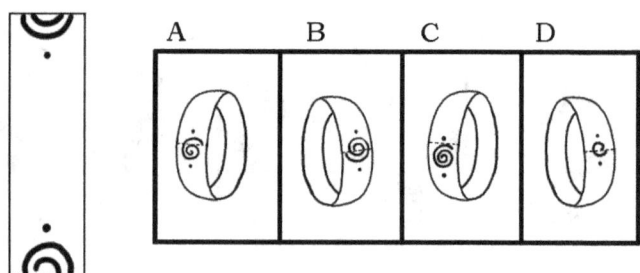

8. Which of the choices is the same pattern at a different angle?

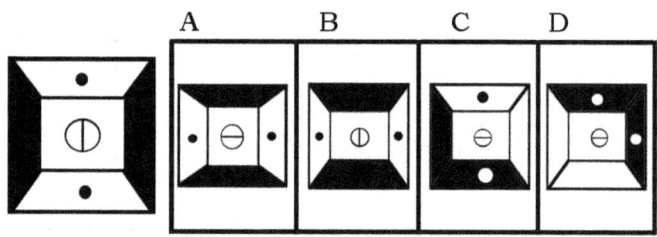

9. When folded, which shape will you get?

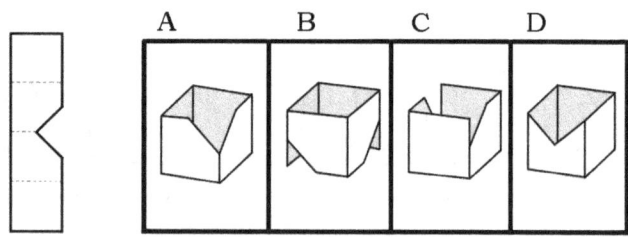

10. When folded, what pattern is possible?

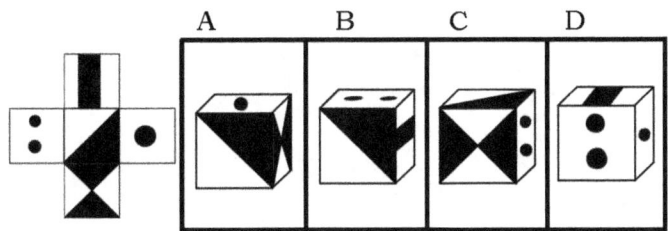

11. Which figure represents the assembly of the following pieces?

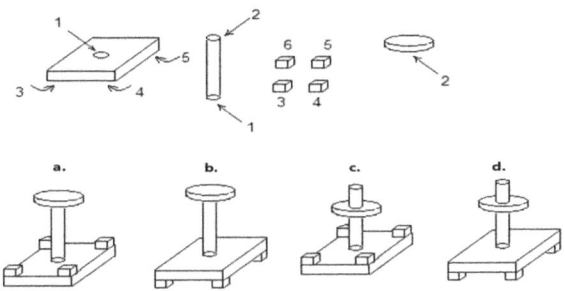

12. Which figure represents the assembly of the following pieces?

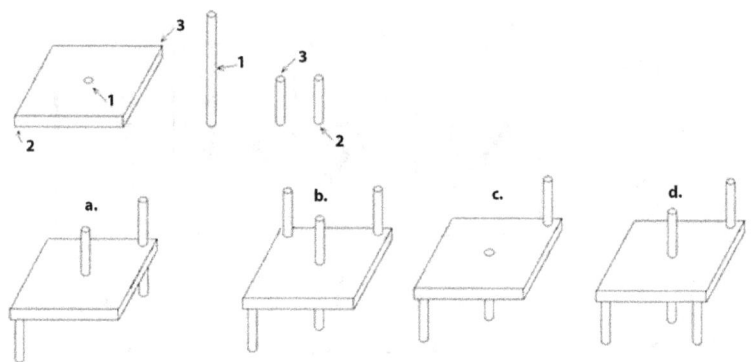

13. Which figure represents the assembly of the following pieces?

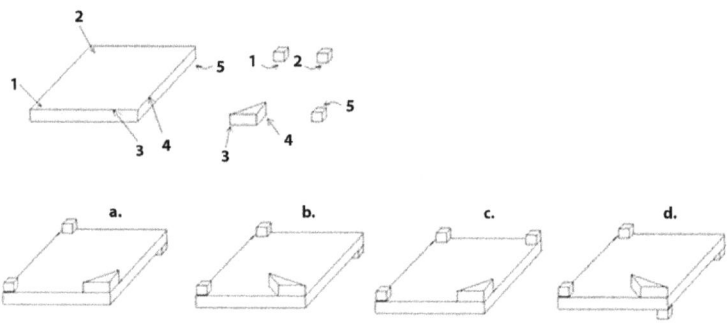

14. Which figure represents the assembly of the following pieces?

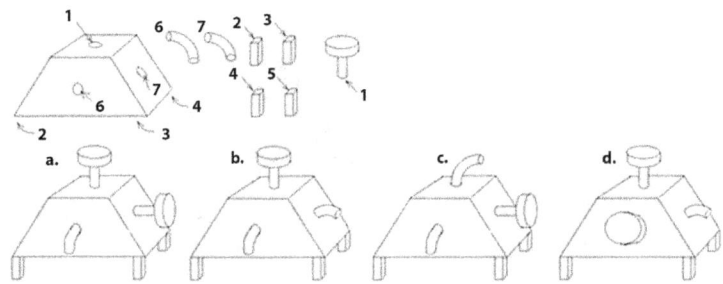

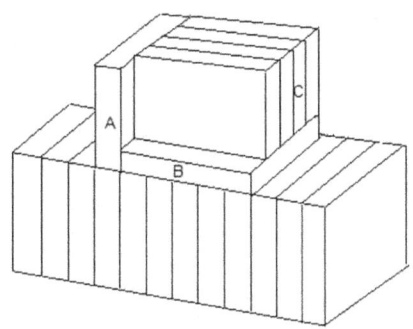

15. How many blocks is block A touching?

    a. 4
    b. 5
    c. 6
    d. 7

16. How many blocks is block B touching?

    a. 4
    b. 5
    c. 9
    d. 10

17. How many cubes are there in the figure?

a. 30
b. 32
c. 35
d. 24

18. How many cubes are there in the figure?

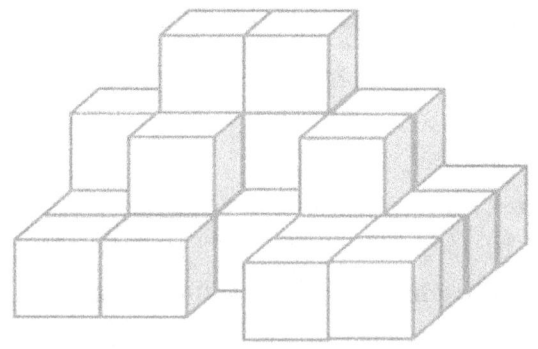

a. 30
b. 22
c. 15
d. 24

19. Which figure is formed by assembling the following pieces?

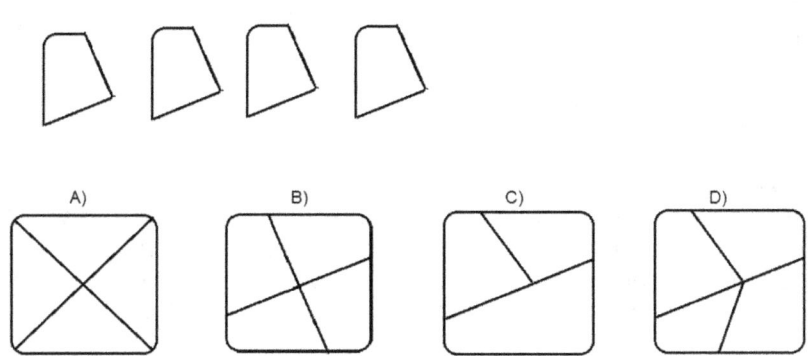

20. Which figure is formed by assembling the following pieces?

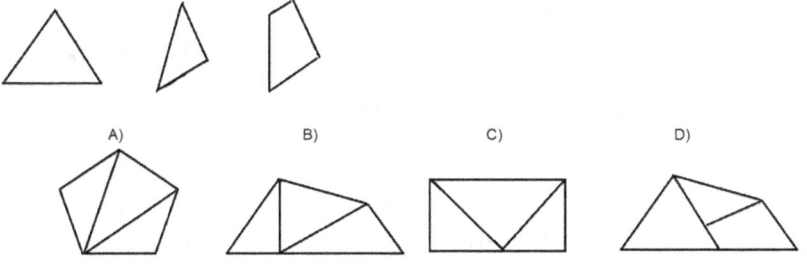

Answer Key

1. D
2. A
3. C
4. B
5. B
6. C
7. B
8. A
9. A
10. A

11. B
If two pieces have the same number at the position shown, it means that point is a junction point. Here, the cylindrical rod is at center of the rectangular platform, the small cubes are below the platform at its edges and the disc is above the rod.

12. D
If two pieces have the same number at the position shown, it means that point is a junction point. Here, the long rod is half above and half below the rectangular platform, and the short rods are one above and the other below the platform.

13. A
If two pieces have the same number at the position shown, it means that point is a junction point. Here, all the small shapes are on the rectangular platform, where the triangular shape is on left-bottom corner and the three small cubes are at the other corners of the platform.

14. B
If two pieces have the same number at the position shown, it means that point is a junction point. Here, the hoses are at the central holes of the lateral faces of the platform, the screw-like shape is on top of the platform and the small cuboids act as legs.

15. C
Block A touches 6 blocks (1 is below, 4 are lateral in vertical position and 1 is lateral in the horizontal position.

16. D
Block B touches 5 blocks below, 4 blocks above and one block laterally, i.e. in total 10 blocks.

17. C
In the bottom row, there are 3 × 4 + 3 = 15 cubes.
In the next row, there are 2 + 3 + 3 + 3 + 1 = 12 cubes.
In the third row, there are 2 + 2 = 4 cubes.
In the upper row, there are only 2 cubes.
Thus, in total there are 15 + 12 + 4 + 2 = 33 cubes.

18. C
From the figure, you will see that there are 4 + 4 + 2 + 3 + 3 = 16 cubes in the bottom row, 2 + 1 + 2 + 1 = 6 cubes in the middle row and only 2 cubes in the upper row.

Thus, in total there are 16 + 6 + 2 = 24 cubes in the figure.

19. B
Since the pieces are identical, only the first two figures can qualify as candidates for the correct answer. The cutting traces in first figure represent the diagonals of the shape. This is not the case here. Hence, only the second figure fits the description.

20. D
There are two triangles and one quadrilateral in the separate pieces. Thus, since all figures except the fourth one contain only triangles, the choice D is the only that fits the description.

Folding Tutorial

For folding questions, you have to mentally manipulate a two-dimensional object by folding it to create a three-dimensional object, and then to identify the resulting object or how it would appear if unfolded.

Folding Spatial Visualization questions are designed to test your ability to mentally manipulate and rotate objects, and understand spatial visualizations and transformations.

To prepare for folding spatial visualization questions, practice visualizing and manipulating two-dimensional and three-dimensional objects in your mind. You can also practice folding paper along different lines and visualizing how the resulting three-dimensional object would appear if unfolded.

Practice will help the most. Below are step-by-step solutions that will help you know what to look for.

With any multiple choice question, the most powerful technique is Elimination.
Look at the choices and eliminate any obviously wrong answers.

Example Questions – TYPE 1

When the two longest sides touch what will the shape be?

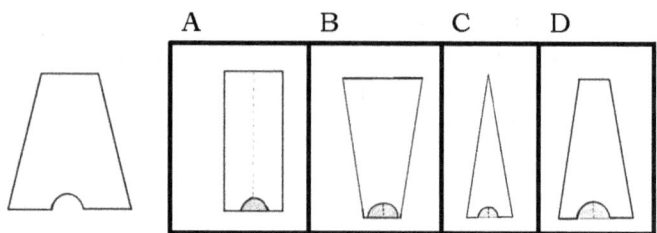

First really look. The given shape has two elements that are distinctive: it is tapered (1) and has a notch at the bottom, which is the widest (2). If this shape is folded, the resulting shape will also be tapered. So, Choice A can be eliminated right away.

Looking at the notch, which is in the widest part, we can see that choice B, which has the notch at the narrowest part, is incorrect
That leaves choices C and D. Looking at choice C, the shape comes to a sharp point. This is impossible with the given shape so choice C can be eliminated.

.Choice D is left. Checking quickly, it is tapered, to flat top and the notch is at the bottom, widest part. Choice D is correct.

Another Example

When folded, what pattern is possible?

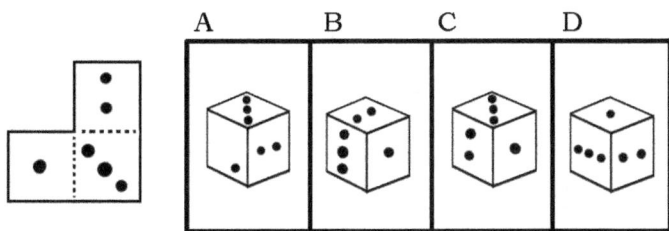

The key here is which sides will be next to each other and which corners will touch. The given figure has one, two and three dots in separate squares that folded, will make a cube with open ends.
Notice that the three dots go from corner to corner, the one dot is in the center, and the two does are up and down in the middle.

Choices B and D can be eliminated, since the three dots are not corner to corner.

That leaves choices A and C. Looking at choice A, the one dot is in the corner, not in the center so choice a can be eliminated.

A More Complex Example

With this type of more complex folding question, look at which sides will be next to each other when folded, and the orientation relative to each other.

A six-sided flat shape will create a cube. This is hard to visualize so keep track of the relations between sides by numbering as below.

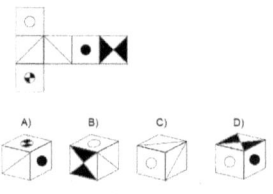

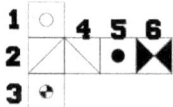

Now, it is easy to visualize adjacent sides

1 and 3
2 and 5
4 and 6

Look at the choices, and orientation of the symbols. Square 6 will never be in position with the wide edge to the white circle, so choice B can be eliminated. Similarly, the white circle can never be in the position relative to the upward and downward lines in choice C. Similarly, with choice A, the dark circle will not be in the position shown, leaving choice D. Choice D has the dark circle positioned at the bottom or thick end of the two triangles, and the white circle at the side.

Another Example

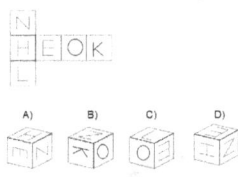

Look at the given shape and number the squares in your heard. Note the orientation relative to what will be an adjacent square when folded into a cube.

Choice A can be eliminated as the N and H are oriented incorrectly. Choice B can be eliminated as the O and K are oriented incorrectly. Choice C looks correct.

Check choice D. Choice D can be eliminated as the N and E are oriented incorrectly.

The Dry Run

Ready to Test Your Skills? Below you will find a full-length practice test. Please note that these are not the exact questions from the official exam—those are kept secret and change every year. Instead, we have created questions that mirror the style and difficulty of the official test.

The Bottom Line: If you can answer these questions correctly, you have the knowledge needed to pass the real exam.

Instructions:

Get in the Zone: Set aside uninterrupted time in a quiet room.

Focus: Read the instructions and every question carefully. Answer to the best of your ability.

Simulate: Use the provided bubble answer sheets to mimic the real test experience.

Review: Once finished, check your work against the Answer Key and read the explanations for any questions you missed.

Pro Tip: Do not attempt more than one practice test in a single day. Rest is just as important as practice. Wait 48 to 72 hours between tests for maximum retention.

Interpreting Written Material

	A B C D E		A B C D E
1	○ ○ ○ ○ ○	21	○ ○ ○ ○ ○
2	○ ○ ○ ○ ○	22	○ ○ ○ ○ ○
3	○ ○ ○ ○ ○	23	○ ○ ○ ○ ○
4	○ ○ ○ ○ ○	24	○ ○ ○ ○ ○
5	○ ○ ○ ○ ○	25	○ ○ ○ ○ ○
6	○ ○ ○ ○ ○		
7	○ ○ ○ ○ ○		
8	○ ○ ○ ○ ○		
9	○ ○ ○ ○ ○		
10	○ ○ ○ ○ ○		
11	○ ○ ○ ○ ○		
12	○ ○ ○ ○ ○		
13	○ ○ ○ ○ ○		
14	○ ○ ○ ○ ○		
15	○ ○ ○ ○ ○		
16	○ ○ ○ ○ ○		
17	○ ○ ○ ○ ○		
18	○ ○ ○ ○ ○		
19	○ ○ ○ ○ ○		
20	○ ○ ○ ○ ○		

Toolbox Math

	A	B	C	D
1	○	○	○	○
2	○	○	○	○
3	○	○	○	○
4	○	○	○	○
5	○	○	○	○
6	○	○	○	○
7	○	○	○	○
8	○	○	○	○
9	○	○	○	○
10	○	○	○	○
11	○	○	○	○
12	○	○	○	○
13	○	○	○	○
14	○	○	○	○
15	○	○	○	○
16	○	○	○	○
17	○	○	○	○
18	○	○	○	○
19	○	○	○	○
20	○	○	○	○

Science

	A	B	C	D
1	○	○	○	○
2	○	○	○	○
3	○	○	○	○
4	○	○	○	○
5	○	○	○	○
6	○	○	○	○
7	○	○	○	○
8	○	○	○	○
9	○	○	○	○
10	○	○	○	○
11	○	○	○	○
12	○	○	○	○
13	○	○	○	○
14	○	○	○	○
15	○	○	○	○
16	○	○	○	○
17	○	○	○	○
18	○	○	○	○
19	○	○	○	○
20	○	○	○	○

Mechanical Systems

	A	B	C	D
1	○	○	○	○
2	○	○	○	○
3	○	○	○	○
4	○	○	○	○
5	○	○	○	○
6	○	○	○	○
7	○	○	○	○
8	○	○	○	○
9	○	○	○	○
10	○	○	○	○
11	○	○	○	○
12	○	○	○	○
13	○	○	○	○
14	○	○	○	○
15	○	○	○	○
16	○	○	○	○
17	○	○	○	○
18	○	○	○	○
19	○	○	○	○
20	○	○	○	○

Spatial Visualization

	A	B	C	D
1	○	○	○	○
2	○	○	○	○
3	○	○	○	○
4	○	○	○	○
5	○	○	○	○
6	○	○	○	○
7	○	○	○	○
8	○	○	○	○
9	○	○	○	○
10	○	○	○	○
11	○	○	○	○
12	○	○	○	○
13	○	○	○	○
14	○	○	○	○
15	○	○	○	○
16	○	○	○	○
17	○	○	○	○
18	○	○	○	○
19	○	○	○	○
20	○	○	○	○

Interpreting Written Material

Directions: The following questions are based on several reading passages. Each passage is followed by a series of questions. Read each passage carefully, and then answer the questions based on it. You may reread the passage as often as you wish. When you have finished answering the questions based on one passage, go right onto the next passage. Choose the best answer based on the information given and implied.

Questions 1 – 4 refer to the following passage.

Mill worker crushed in winder
Steve and Jonathon are childhood friends and went to school together. Both were well known athletes in school, and played high school football. They have been working in a same mill for the last 25 years. Jonathan is considered to be one of the best footballers in the school. Similarly, he became a jack of all trades in his workplace withy complete knowledge of every process involved in the mill. Whenever management found a problem with any of the machines, or a way to improve a work procedure, they called on Jonathan first. His suggestions were always considered and most of the time, followed by management. He was the 'go-to-guy' to get things done at the mill

Due to his experience and familiarity with the machines and maintenance, Jonathan was very confident and often considered himself above the rules and regulations related to employee safety developed by the management and implemented by the Health and Safety department of the company. Management did not take any serious action on this because of Jonathan's rank and senior position in organization. One day, when he neglected the safety rules while doing maintenance on a winder. Walking the shop in his free time, Steve went through the area where winder was installed. He saw that Jonathan was working on the winder and had removed the safety guards. Since some of the newer young workers were standing nearby. Steve thought Jonathan was teaching them how to service the winder, as he had done to Steve when he joined the company.

Steve suddenly noticed the intake of the winder was not locked. The intake should always be locked when the safety guards of the winder are removed, according to the workplace safety rules and regulations. At first, Steve thought of correcting Jonathan, but considered his own position, experience and qualifications. He thought to himself, "Who am I to correct such an experienced person in front of new hires when he is training. Would that be appropriate to ask him about following the safety procedures?" He also considered it was possible that Jonathan has developed another safe method to do maintenance of winder. He shook his head and continued walking through the area. After some time, he heard winder start up.

Next, he heard the sound of the winder change, and the workers shouting. He turned around and saw that a person was stuck in the winder. He ran towards the winder in a panic and saw that Jonathan had been pulled into the winder up to his waist. He was trying to pull him out, but couldn't. According to the emergency protocols developed by the management and safety officials, Steve immediately moved towards the E stop button and pushed it. He again came back and tried to pull him out. By the time he had pulled him out, Jonathan was seriously injured. He was taken to the hospital but could not be saved.

1. How long have Steve and Jonathan known each other?

      a. 25 years

      b. Less than 25 years

      c. More than 25 years

      d. None of the above

2. Who did management call for suggestions when any critical situation occurred?

    a. Steve

    b. Jonathan

    c. None of them

    d. Both of them

3. Jonathan always follow by the rules?

    a. Yes

    b. No

4. Why didn't management take any action against him?

    a. Due to his rank

    b. Due to his experience

    c. Both A and B

    d. None of the above

5. What was Jonathan doing when the accident occurred?

    a. Standing idle

    b. Doing maintenance on a shaft

    c. Doing maintenance on a winder

    d. None of the above

6. Who saw Jonathan (aside from the new workers) when he was doing maintenance?

    a. No one

    b. Steve

    c. Safety inspector

    d. He was alone

7. Why didn't Steve correct Jonathan?

  a. He thought of his rank and experience
  b. To take revenge
  c. He did corrected Jonathan
  d. None of the above

8. Who is your opinion is responsible for this accident?

  a. Steve
  b. Jonathan
  c. Management
  d. All of these

Questions 9 – 11 refer to the following passage.

Instruction Manual Excerpt: Portable Cement Mixer

Operating Instructions:

Place the mixer on stable, level ground before adding materials.

Connect the mixer to a grounded electrical outlet.

Add gravel and sand before adding water. Cement powder should be added last.

Do not exceed the maximum fill line marked inside the drum.

Allow the drum to rotate for 3–5 minutes before pouring.

Shut off power and clean the drum immediately after use to prevent hardened buildup.

9. According to the instructions, what must be done first before operating the cement mixer?

    a. Add gravel and sand to the drum

    b. Place the mixer on stable, level ground

    c. Connect the mixer to an extension cord

    d. Add water to test rotation

10. In what order should materials be added?

    a. Water → cement → gravel

    b. Cement → sand → water

    c. Gravel and sand → water → cement

    d. Cement → water → sand

11. Why must the drum be cleaned immediately after use?

    a. To avoid contaminating the next batch of cement

    b. To prevent hardened material from building up

    c. To reduce electrical strain on the motor

    d. To ensure accurate measurement of sand

Questions 12 – 15 refer to the following passage.

A Glimpse into a Vital Trade

Jake is a licensed electrician who spends his days installing and repairing electrical systems in homes and offices. One morning, he was called to a client's house because the lights kept flickering in the living room. After carefully inspecting the wiring, Jake discovered that the issue was caused by a loose wire connection in the circuit breaker panel. He tightened the connection and tested the lights, which no longer flickered. Jake also noticed an old electrical outlet that was slightly discolored and recommended replacing it to prevent future problems. The homeowners were relieved and grateful for Jake's attention to detail and expertise.

12. What problem did Jake fix for the homeowners?

    a. A leaky faucet

    b. Flickering lights

    c. Broken window

    d. Clogged drain

13. Based on the passage, what does "discolored" most likely mean in the context of the electrical outlet?

    a. Bright and shiny

    b. Unusually colored or stained

    c. New and clean

    d. Covered in dust

14. Why did Jake recommend replacing the old electrical outlet?

    a. To make the room look better

    b. To match the furniture

    c. To prevent future problems

    d. Because the homeowners asked him to

15. What can you infer about Jake's work habits?

    a. He is careless

    b. He is detail-oriented

    c. He is always late

    d. He dislikes his job

Questions 16 – 19 refer to the following passage.

Equipment Maintenance Log Entry

Equipment: Pneumatic Torque Wrench
Inspection Date: February 14
Inspector: R. Chan

Findings:

Air hose shows signs of minor cracking near the connection point.

Torque output reading fluctuates by 5–7% during operation.

No leakage detected.

Action Taken:

Hose marked for replacement before next scheduled use.

Recommend recalibration of torque mechanism.
Next Review: After hose replacement or within 30 days.

16. What issue was identified with the air hose?

    a. It was leaking air during operation

    b. It showed cracking near the connection

    c. It had a loose clamp and required tightening

    d. It was too short for proper tool reach

17. What does the fluctuating torque reading suggest?

    a. The wrench is operating normally

    b. The hose length is incorrect

    c. The torque mechanism needs recalibration

    d. The tool is overheating

18. According to the log, when should the next review occur?

    a. Immediately, before the hose is replaced

    b. Only after recalibration

    c. After the hose is replaced or within 30 days

    d. Only if a leak develops

19. Which action was taken during the inspection?

    a. The hose was replaced

    b. The torque wrench was recalibrated

    c. The hose was marked for replacement

    d. The tool was taken out of service entirely

Questions 20 - 23 refer to the following recipe.

Safety Bulletin: Working in Confined Spaces

A confined space is any area that is not designed for continuous occupancy and has limited entry and exit points. Before entering a confined space, workers must complete an atmospheric test for oxygen levels, flammable gases, and toxic vapours. Continuous monitoring is required if any readings are close to the acceptable limits.

Workers must wear appropriate personal protective equipment (PPE), including a harness connected to a retrieval system. A trained attendant must remain outside the confined space at all times to monitor conditions and initiate rescue procedures if necessary.

No worker may enter the confined space unless an entry permit has been completed, signed, and visibly posted at the work site.

20. What must be done before entering a confined space?

   a. Turn off all surrounding equipment

   b. Complete atmospheric testing

   c. Install new lighting in the space

   d. Conduct a toolbox meeting with all site workers

21. Why is continuous monitoring required?

   a. To track worker productivity

   b. Because atmospheric levels may change

   c. To ensure communication equipment is functioning

   d. Because workers must update the entry permit every hour

22. What role does the attendant play?

   a. They assist with tasks inside the confined space

   b. They decide what tools should be used

   c. They monitor conditions and initiate rescue if needed

   d. They sign the entry permit on behalf of the supervisor

23. Which document must be visibly posted before anyone enters?

   a. The equipment maintenance log

   b. A completed and signed entry permit

   c. A lockout/tagout checklist

   d. The worker's training certificate

Questions 24 – 25 refer to the following email.

SUBJECT: STAFF CHANGES

To all staff:

This email is to advise you of a paper on recommended medical staff changes has been posted to the Human Resources website.

The contents are of primary interest to plant staff, other staff may be interested in reading it, particularly those in medical support roles.

The paper deals with several major issues:

    1. Improving our ability to attract top quality staff to the hospital, and retain our existing staff. These changes will make our position and departmental names internationally recognizable and comparable with North American and North Asian departments and positions.

    2. Improving our ability to attract top quality staff by introducing greater flexibility in the departmental structure.

    3. General comments on issues to be further discussed relative to research staff.

The changes outlined in this paper are significant. I encourage you to read the document and send to me any comments you may have, so that it can be enhanced and improved.

Gordon Simms
Administrator

24. Are all hospital staff required to read the document posted to the Human Resources website?

    a. Yes all staff are required to read the document.

    b. No, reading the document is optional.

    c. Only medical staff are required to read the document.

    d. none of the above are correct.

25. Have the changes to medical staff been made?

    a. Yes, the changes have been made.

    b. No, the changes are only being discussed.

    c. Some of the changes have been made.

    d. None of the choices are correct.

Toolbox Math

Part 1: Whole Numbers & Order of Operations

1. A contractor buys 12 sheets of plywood at 45 each, 5 boxes of screws at 12 each, and a drill for 120. What is the total cost before tax?

    a. 660

    b. 720

    c. 177

    d. 780

2. Evaluate the following expression: $20 + 4 \times (12 - 5)$.

    a. 168

    b. 48

    c. 37

    d. 88

3. An electrician cuts three pieces of wire from a 50-foot spool. The pieces are 8 feet, 12 feet, and 15 feet long. How much wire is left on the spool?

    a. 15 feet
    b. 35 feet
    c. 25 feet
    d. 18 feet

Part 2: Fractions

4. A carpenter needs to cut a board that is 15 3/4 inches long from a piece that is 24 1/2 inches long. How much wood will remain (ignoring the saw kerf)?

    a. 9 1/4 inches
    b. 8 3/4 inches
    c. 8 1/2 inches
    d. 9 3/4 inches

5. A recipe for mortar calls for 2/3 of a bucket of sand. If you need to make 6 batches, how many buckets of sand do you need?

    a. 3 buckets
    b. 4 buckets
    c. 3 1/3 buckets
    d. 9 buckets

6. Which of the following fractions is the largest?

    a. 5/8
    b. 1/2
    c. 3/4
    d. 9/16

7. Convert 5/16 to a decimal.

   a. 0.3125
   b. 0.325
   c. 0.255
   d. 0.516

Part 3: Decimals & Percentages

8. A pipe has an outside diameter of 2.85 inches and a wall thickness of 0.125 inches. What is the inside diameter of the pipe?

   a. 2.725 inches
   b. 2.60 inches
   c. 2.975 inches
   d. 2.50 inches

9. A welder purchases equipment for 1,250. If the sales tax is 13%, what is the total cost?

   a. 1,412.50
   b. 1,375.00
   c. 1,263.00
   d. 1,625.50

10. A worker's hourly wage is increased from 20.00 to 23.00. What is the percentage increase?

   a. 10%
   b. 13%
   c. 15%
   d. 20%

Part 4: Ratios & Proportions

11. A concrete mix requires 1 part cement, 2 parts sand, and 3 parts gravel. If you use 4 shovels of cement, how many shovels of gravel are needed?

    a. 8
    b. 10
    c. 12
    d. 6

12. On a blueprint, the scale is 1/4 inch} = 1 foot. If a wall measures 3.5 inches on the blueprint, what is the actual length of the wall?

    a. 12 feet
    b. 14 feet
    c. 10.5 feet
    d. 15 feet

13. A machine produces 150 parts in 2.5 hours. At this rate, how many parts will it produce in 8 hours?

    a. 400
    b. 450
    c. 480
    d. 600

Part 5: Measurement Conversion

14. How many inches are in 6 feet 4 inches?

    a. 64 inches
    b. 72 inches
    c. 76 inches
    d. 78 inches

15. Convert 3.5 meters to millimeters.

    a. 350 mm

    b. 3,500 mm

    c. 35 mm

    d. 0.0035 mm

16. A tank holds 5 gallons of liquid. Approx how many liters is this? (Use 1 gallon approx 3.78 liters)

    a. 15.6 liters

    b. 18.9 liters

    c. 22.1 liters

    d. 12.5 liters

Part 6: Geometry (Perimeter, Area, Volume)

17. Calculate the perimeter of a rectangular room that measures 12 feet by 15 feet.

    a. 27 feet

    b. 54 feet

    c. 180 feet

    d. 60 feet

18. What is the area of a triangle with a base of 10 inches and a height of 8 inches?

    a. 80 sq inches

    b. 18 sq inches

    c. 40 sq inches

    d. 36 sq inches

19. A cylindrical tank has a radius of 3 feet and a height of 10 feet. What is the volume? (Use pi approx 3.14)

    a. 94.2 cubic feet

    b. 282.6 cubic feet

    c. 188.4 cubic feet

    d. 31.4 cubic feet

20. Find the hypotenuse of a right-angled triangle with legs measuring 6 cm and 8 cm.

    a. 10 cm

    b. 12 cm

    c. 14 cm

    d. 9 cm

Science

1. _____, which refers to the repeatability of measurement, does not require knowledge of the correct or true value.

    a. Precision

    b. Value

    c. Certainty

    d. Accuracy

2. Describe the periodic table.

a. The periodic table is a tabular display of the chemical compounds organized on the basis of their atomic numbers, electron configurations, and recurring chemical properties.

b. The periodic table is a tabular display of the chemical elements, organized on the basis of their atomic numbers, electron configurations, and recurring chemical properties.

c. The periodic table is a tabular display of the chemical subatomic particles, organized on the basis of their atomic numbers, electron configurations, and recurring chemical properties.

d. None of the above.

3. In terms of the scientific method, the term _____ refers to the act of noticing or perceiving something and/or recording a fact or occurrence.

a. Observation
b. Diligence
c. Perception
d. Control

4. What is the difference, of any, between kinetic energy and potential energy?

a. Kinetic energy is the energy of a body that results from heat while potential energy is the energy possessed by an object that is chilled

b. Kinetic energy is the energy of a body that results from motion while potential energy is the energy possessed by an object by virtue of its position or state, e.g., as in a compressed spring.

c. There is no difference between kinetic and potential energy; all energy is the same.

d. Potential energy is the energy of a body that results from motion while kinetic energy is the energy possessed by an object by virtue of its position or state, e.g., as in a compressed spring.

5. The scientific term _____ refers to a practical test designed with the intention that its results be relevant to a particular theory or set of theories.

   a. Procedure
   b. Variable
   c. Hypothesis
   d. Experiment

6. Describe kinetic energy.

   a. Kinetic energy is the energy an object possesses due to its mass.
   b. Kinetic energy is the energy an object possesses due to its motion.
   c. Kinetic energy is the energy an object possesses due to its chemical properties.
   d. Kinetic energy is the stored energy an object possesses.

7. The interval of confidence around the measured value, such that the measured value is certain not to lie outside this stated interval, refers to the _____ of that value.

   a. Accuracy
   b. Error
   c. Uncertainty
   d. Measurement

8. A metal rod becomes noticeably longer when heated. What scientific principle explains this?

   a. Thermal contraction
   b. Thermal expansion
   c. Electrical resistance
   d. Magnetic induction

9. A worker uses a 2 m ramp to raise a heavy tool box by 0.5 m. What is the mechanical advantage of the ramp?

    a. 0.25
    b. 1
    c. 2
    d. 4

10. If voltage stays the same but resistance increases, what happens to current? (Ohm's Law)

    a. Current increases
    b. Current decreases
    c. Current stays the same
    d. Current doubles

11. A 12-kg object is pushed with a force of 36 N. What is its acceleration?

    a. 2 m/s^2
    b. 3 m/s^2
    c. 12 m/s^2
    d. 48 m/s^2

12. Why is copper often used for electrical wiring?

    a. It has high resistance
    b. It is a poor heat conductor
    c. It is highly conductive and flexible
    d. It is magnetic

13. A container has a pressure gauge reading 200 kPa. If the temperature increases, what happens to the pressure (closed container)?

    a. Pressure increases
    b. Pressure decreases
    c. Pressure becomes zero
    d. Pressure stays constant

14. What happens to the density of water when it freezes?

    a. It increases
    b. It decreases
    c. It stays the same
    d. It becomes zero

15. A worker uses a pulley system that allows him to lift a 200-kg load using only 100 kg of force. What is the mechanical advantage?

    a. 0.5
    b. 1
    c. 2
    d. 4

16. Which material is the best thermal insulator?

    a. Copper
    b. Aluminum
    c. Wood
    d. Steel

17. When mixing two chemicals, the container becomes warm. What type of reaction is this?

   a. Endothermic
   b. Exothermic
   c. Neutral
   d. Radioactive

18. A board measures 2.5 m in length. How many centimeters is this?

   a. 25 cm
   b. 250 cm
   c. 2,500 cm
   d. 0.25 cm

19. Why does a steel beam feel colder to touch than a wooden board at the same room temperature?

   a. Steel is colder
   b. Wood generates heat
   c. Steel conducts heat away from your hand faster
   d. Wood contains warm air pockets

20. A worker needs to reduce friction between two metal parts. What should be applied?

   a. Water
   b. Sand
   c. Lubricant
   d. Paint

Mechanical Systems

1. Which of the following is an example of torque?

    a. The wheel of a pulley turning
    b. A piston moving
    c. A horse pulling a load
    d. A tow truck pulling a vehicle

2. Find the weight of load L in N, if the pulling force F = 20N.

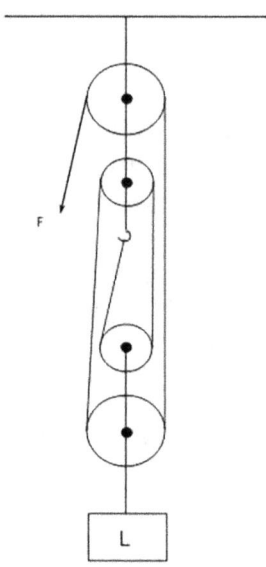

    a. 5
    b. 100
    c. 20
    d. 80

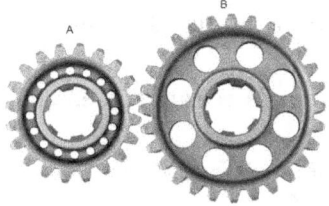

3. How many turns does the gear B make when the gear A makes 14 complete turns?

    a. 8
    b. 10
    c. 20
    d. 28

4. Which of the following is true about the system of meshed gears shown?

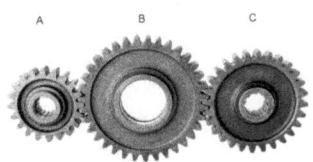

    a. Gear A rotates slower than gear B
    b. Gear A rotates slower than gear C
    c. Gear B rotates slower than gear C
    d. Gear B rotates faster than the other two gears

5. Which of the following is true of the relationship between screws and threads?

    a. The larger the distance between threads, the easier to turn.

    b. The smaller the distance between threads, the easier to turn.

    c. The smaller the distance between threads, the more difficult to turn.

    d. None of the above

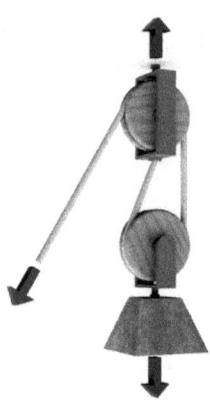

6. Consider the arrangement of pulleys above. If the weight shown is 150 pounds, how much force much be exerted to lift the weight?

    a. 150 pounds

    b. 100 pounds

    c. 75 pounds

    d. 50 pounds

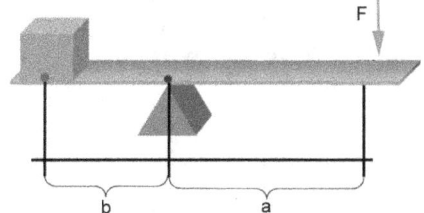

7. Consider the illustration above and the corresponding data:

Weight = W = 100 pounds
Distance from fulcrum to Weight = b = 5 feet
Distance from fulcrum to point where force is applied = a = 10 feet
How much force (F) must be applied to lift the weight?

    a. 100
    b. 50
    c. 25
    d. 10

8. Consider a gear train with 3 gears, from left to right, A with 10 teeth, gear B with 40 teeth, and gear C with 10 teeth. Gear A turns clockwise at 80 rpm. What direction and speed in rpm does Gear C turn?

    a. 100 rpm, clockwise
    b. 80 rpm clockwise
    c. 120 rpm counter clockwise
    d. 100 rpm counter clockwise

9. A force of 40 kg. is applied to two springs in parallel, which compresses the springs 10 inches. If the same force is applied to springs in series, how far will the springs compress?

    a. 40 inches
    b. 5 inches
    c. 10 inches
    d. 5 inches

10. Tension of 40 kg. is applied to two springs in series, which expand the springs 20 inches. If the same amount of tension is applied to springs in parallel, how far will the springs expand?

    a. 20 inches
    b. 10 inches
    c. 5 inches
    d. 2 inch

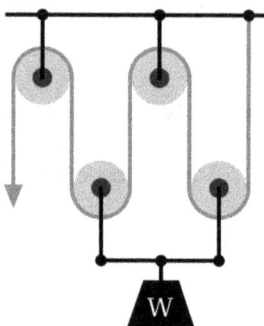

11. Consider the pulley arrangement above. If the weight, W, is 100 pounds, then how much force is required to lift the weight?

    a. 100 pounds
    b. 50 pounds
    c. 25 pounds
    d. 20 pounds

12. A cam is a mechanical linkage that:

a. Transforms linear motion into rotary motion and vice versa.

b. Transforms oscillating motion in to linear motion and vice versa.

c. Transforms reciprocating motion to oscillating motion.

d. None of the above

13. What is the function of the crankshaft?

a. To transform the back-and-forth motion of the pistons into rotary motion.

b. To transform rotary motion into reciprocal motion.

c. To transfer the rotary motion of the cam to the wheels

d. None of the above.

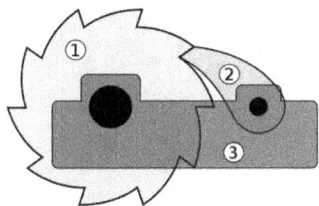

14. Identify the components labeled above.

a. 1 - ratchet, 2 - pawl, 3 - base

b. 1 - pawl, 2 - ratchet, 3 - base

c. 1 - gear, 2 - stop, 3 base

d. None of the above

15. Which equation below shows the relationship between F and P for the system of pulleys shown?

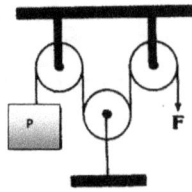

a. P = 3F
b. P = 2F
c. P = F
d. P = F/2

16. How many newtons of force is needed to pull the object up an inclined plane, if the weight of the object is 200 N?

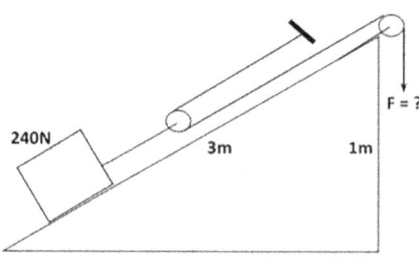

a. 50
b. 100
c. 150
d. 200

17. What is the force applied to lift the 400 N weight shown?

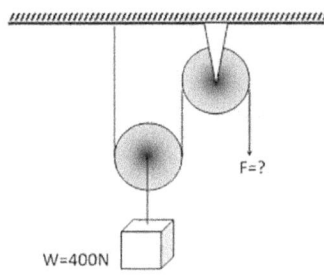

a. 200 N
b. 300 N
c. 400 N
d. 800 N

18. How many turns does gear 1 make when gear 3 makes 210 turns?

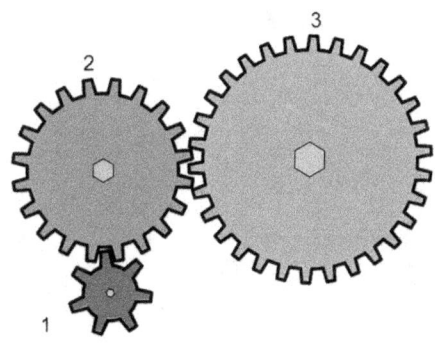

a. 30
b. 90
c. 300
d. 900

19. What is the minimum force (in N) needed to lift the 600 N object, if x = 3 m and y = 2 m?

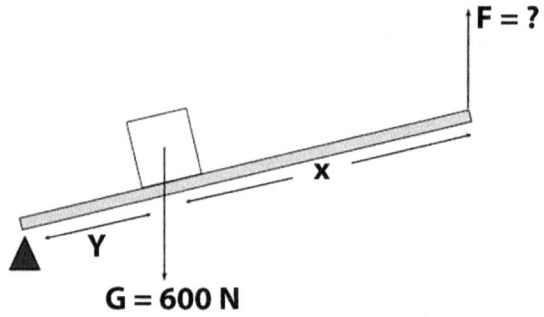

a. 400
b. 320
c. 240
d. 180

20. What is the distance between the mass m and the fulcrum, if the system is in equilibrium and the length of the rod d is 120 cm? Give the answer in cm.

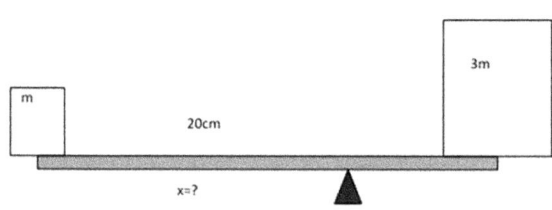

a. 80
b. 85
c. 90
d. 95

Spatial Visualization

1. When folded, which shape is possible?

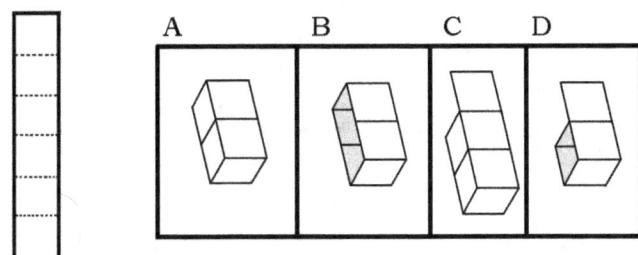

2. When folded, what pattern is possible?

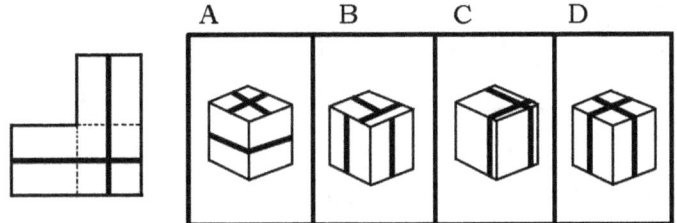

3. When folded into a loop, what will the strip of paper look like?

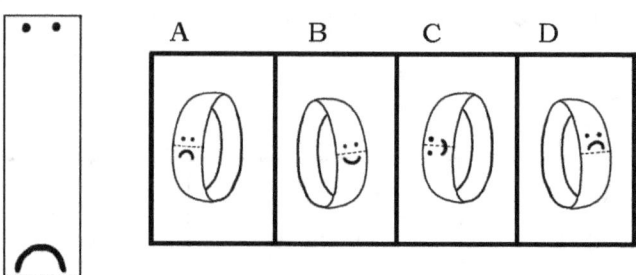

4. Which of the choices is the same pattern at a different angle?

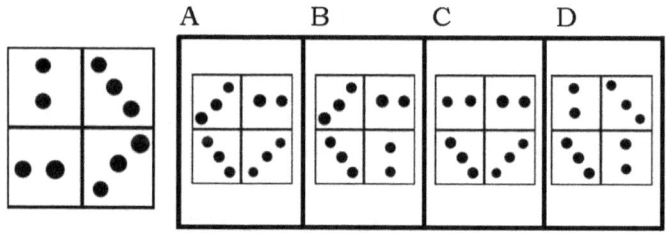

5. When folded along the dotted lines, which shape will you get?

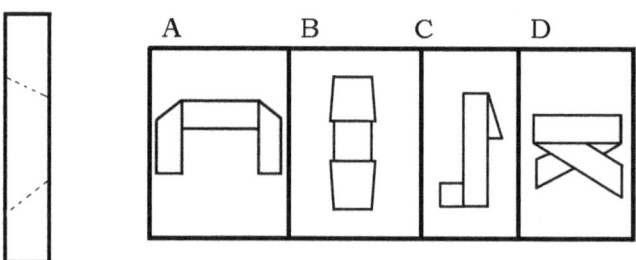

6. When folded, what pattern is possible?

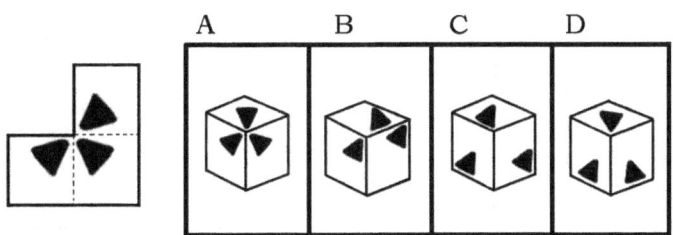

7. When folded into a loop, what will the strip of paper look like?

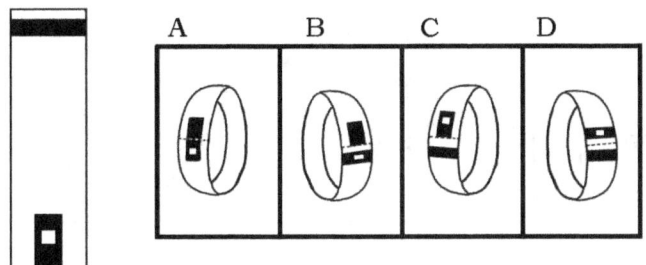

8. Which of the choices is the same pattern at a different angle?

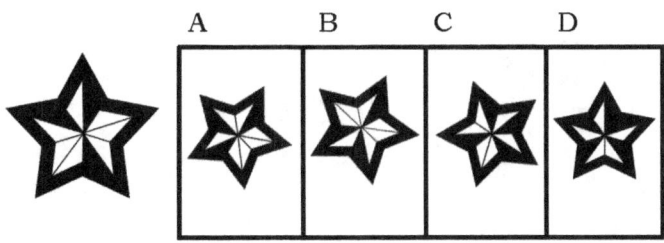

9. When folded along the dotted line, which shape will you get?

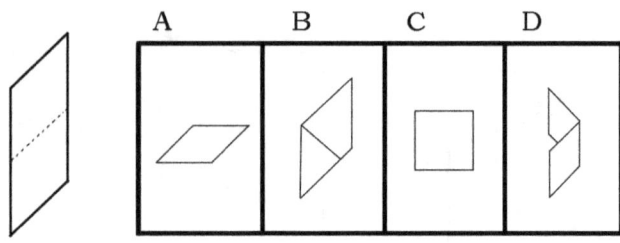

10. When folded, what pattern is possible?

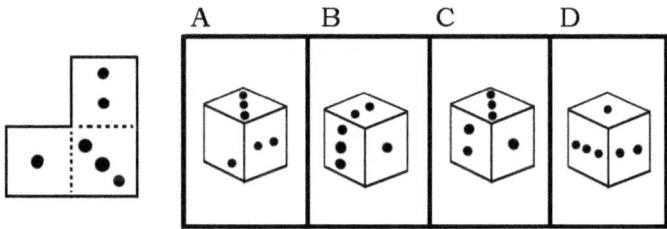

11. Which figure represents the assembly of the following pieces?

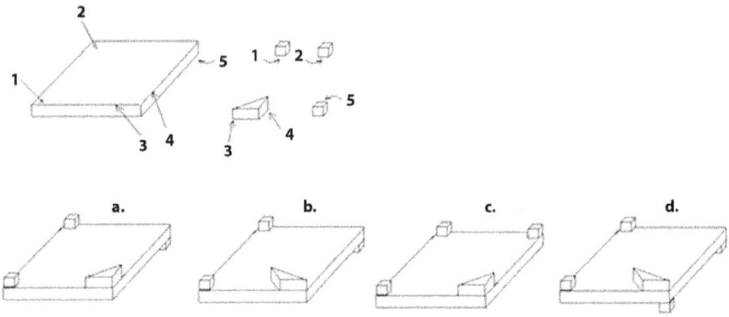

12. Which figure represents the assembly of the following pieces?

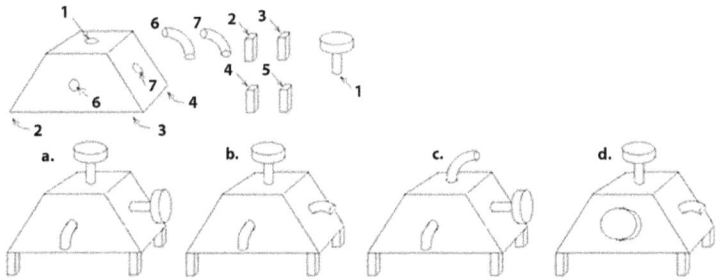

13. Which figure represents the assembly of the following pieces?

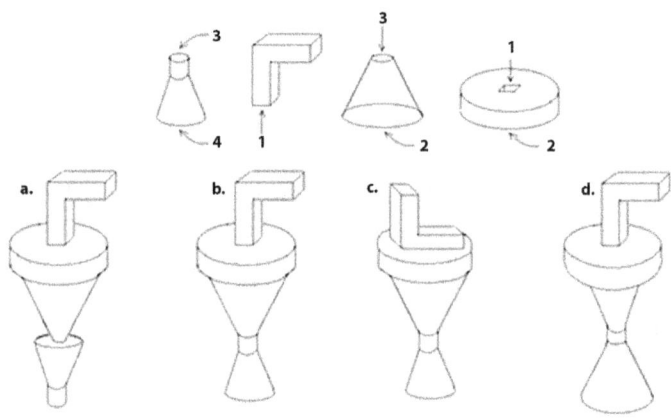

Questions 14 - 16 refer to the following diagram

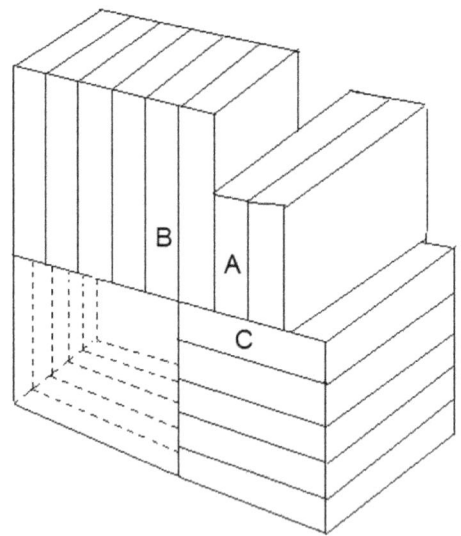

**14. How many blocks is block A in the figure touching?
The blocks on the bottom-left side are transparent.**

   a. 6
   b. 5
   c. 4
   d. 3

**15. How many blocks is block B in the figure touching?
The blocks on the bottom-left side are transparent.**

   a. 7
   b. 6
   c. 5
   d. 4

**16. How many blocks is block B in the figure touching?
The blocks on the bottom-left side are transparent.**

   a. 10
   b. 9
   c. 8
   d. 7

17. How many small cubes are missing in the figure to form a large perfect cube?

a. 6
b. 7
c. 8
d. 9

18. Which shape must we place on the existing figure to form a perfect cube?

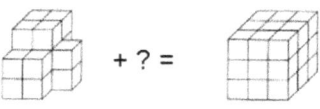

A) 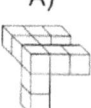   B)    C) 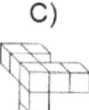   D)

19. Which shape must we place on the existing figure to form a perfect cube?

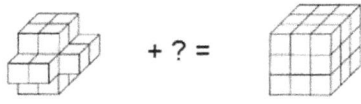

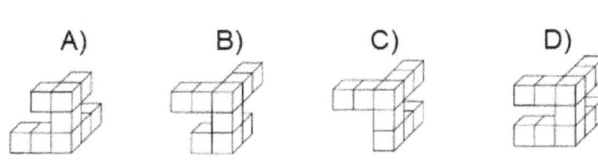

20. Which shape must we place on the existing figure to form a perfect cube?

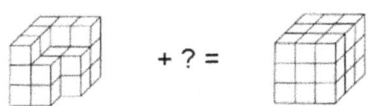

Answer Key

Interpreting Written Material

1. C
They have known each other since childhood and worked at the same company for 25 years.
Choice A is closed associated but not correct because their relationships is for more than 25 years
Choice B is incorrect because they know each other more than 25 years

2. B
Jonathan was expert on all the processes and machines in the mill

3. B
He felt he was so experienced he could neglect the safety rules

4. C
Jonathan enjoyed a higher status because of his rank and experience in the mill
Choice A is incorrect because his rank was not the only issue but his experience also
Choice B is incorrect because not only his experience but also his rank were an issue

5. C
He was teaching new workers about winder maintenance
Choice A is incorrect because he was working
Choice B is incorrect. There is no mention of a shaft.
Choice D is irrelevant

6. B
His friend Steve saw him while he was walking through the area
Choice A is irrelevant because he was teaching the newcomers.
Choice C is incorrect because no safety inspector was present there.
Choice D is incorrect because there were a lot of newcomers

standing beside him

7. A
Steve remained quiet while thinking about his position and experience.
Choice B is incorrect. He was not angry with him
Choice C is incorrect. He did not correct him

8. D
All of them are either directly or indirectly responsible for this accident
Choice A is incorrect because he alone is not responsible
Choice B is incorrect because he alone is not responsible
Choice C is incorrect because management alone is not responsible

9. B
None of the statements are the author's opinion.

10. A
The author's purpose is the inform.

11. A
The only statement that is not a detail is, "A doctor can diagnosis this medical condition by asking the patient questions and testing."

12. B
Jake was called to fix the flickering lights in the living room. The other options (leaky faucet, broken window, clogged drain) are not mentioned in the passage.

13. B
The word "discolored" in the context of an electrical outlet means it looks stained or has abnormal coloring, possibly due to age or damage. The outlet is not bright and shiny (A), new and clean (C), or simply covered in dust (D).

14. C
Jake recommended replacing the outlet to avoid potential issues. The passage doesn't mention appearance (A), matching furniture (B), or a request from homeowners (D).
  B) He is detail-oriented

Jake notices a problem that the homeowners did not mention and recommends a solution, showing attention to detail. There is no evidence he is careless (A), always late (C), or dislikes his job (D).

15. B

The log states "minor cracking near the connection."

16. C

Fluctuating torque indicates recalibration is needed.

17. C

Next review: hose replacement or 30 days.

18. C

The hose was marked for replacement, not yet replaced.

19. B

Atmospheric testing is required before entry.

20. B

Conditions can change, so ongoing monitoring is needed.

21. C

The attendant monitors and can initiate rescue procedures.

22. B

A signed entry permit must be posted.

23. D

This question tests the reader's global understanding of the text. Choice D includes the main topics of the three body paragraphs, and isn't too focused on a specific aspect or quote from the text, as the other questions are, giving a skewed summary of what the author intended. The reader may be drawn to choice B because of the title of the passage and the use of words like "better," but the message of the passage is larger and more general than this.

24. B

Reading the document posted to the Human Resources website is optional.

25. B
The document is recommended changes and have not be implemented yet.

Toolbox Math

1. Correct Answer: B $720
Step 1: Calculate the cost of the plywood:
12 {sheets} X 45 = 540.
Step 2: Calculate the cost of the screws:
5 boxes X 12 = 60.
Step 3: Add the cost of the drill: 120.
Step 4: Sum the totals: 540 + 60 + 120 = 720.

2. Correct Answer: B (48)
Step 1: Follow BEDMAS/PEMDAS (Brackets first). Solve inside the parentheses: (12 - 5) = 7.
Step 2: Perform multiplication next: 4 X 7 = 28.
Step 3: Perform addition last: 20 + 28 = 48.
Student Pitfall: Adding 20 and 4 first (getting 24) and then multiplying by 7, which gives the incorrect answer of 168.

3. Correct Answer: A (15 feet)
Step 1: Add the lengths of the cut pieces: 8 + 12 + 15 = 35 feet.
Step 2: Subtract the total cut amount from the spool length: 50 - 35 = 15 feet.

4. Correct Answer: B (8 3/4 inches)
Step 1: Set up the subtraction: 4 1/2 - 15 3/4.
Step 2: Find a common denominator for the fractions 1/2 and 3/4. The common denominator is 4. Convert 1/2 to 2/4.
Step 3: Now you have 24 2/4 - 15 3/4. You cannot subtract 3 from 2, so you must borrow 1 whole from the 24.
Step 4: Rewrite 24 as 23 + 4/4. Add that to the fraction: 23 6/4 - 15 3/4.
Step 5: Subtract whole numbers: 23 - 15 = 8. Subtract fractions: 6/4 - 3/4 = 3/4.
Step 6: Combine: 8 3/4 inches.
Student Pitfall: Subtracting the smaller fraction from the larger regardless of order (i.e., doing 3/4 - 2/4 leading to answer A (9 1/4).

5. Correct Answer: B (4 buckets)
Step 1: Set up the multiplication: 2/3 X 6/1.
Step 2: Turn the whole number into a fraction: 2/3 X 6/1.
Step 3: Multiply numerators and denominators: 2 X 6 3 X 1 = 12/3.
Step 4: Simplify: 12 \ 3 = 4.

6. Correct Answer: C 3/4
Step 1: Convert all fractions to a common denominator (16 is the easiest).

5/8 = 10/16
1/2 = 8/16
3/4 = 12/16
9/16 = 9/16

Step 2: Compare numerators: 12 is the highest. Therefore, 3/4 is the largest.

7. Correct Answer: A (0.3125)
Step 1: To convert a fraction to a decimal, divide the numerator (5) by the denominator (16).
Step 2: 5 \ 16 = 0.3125.

8. Correct Answer: B (2.60 inches)
Step 1: Understand that the outside diameter includes the wall thickness on both sides of the pipe.
Step 2: Calculate total wall thickness to subtract: 0.125 + 0.125 = 0.250 inches.
Step 3: Subtract from Outside Diameter (OD): 2.85 - 0.25 = 2.60 inches.
Student Pitfall: Subtracting the wall thickness only once (2.85 - 0.125), leading to answer A (2.725).

9. Correct Answer: A ($1,412.50)
Step 1: Calculate the tax amount:
1,250 X 0.13 = 162.50.
Step 2: Add tax to the original price:
1,250 + 162.50 = 1,412.50.
Alternative Step: Multiply directly by 1.13:
1250 X 1.13 = 1412.5.

10. Correct Answer: C (15%)
Step 1: Find the difference in wage: 23 - 20 = $3.00.
Step 2: Divide the difference by the original amount: 3/20.
Step 3: Convert to percentage: 3/20 X 100 = 0.15 X 100 = 15%.
Student Pitfall: Dividing by the new amount 3 \ 23, resulting in approx 13%.

11. Correct Answer: C (12)
Step 1: Identify the ratio of Cement to Gravel - 1:3.
Step 2: Set up the proportion:
1 (cement) / 3 (gravel = 4 \ (cement) / x (gravel).
Step 3: Cross multiply or observe the multiplier:
1 X 4 = 4, so 3 X 4 = 12.

12. Correct Answer: B (14 feet)
Step 1: Determine how many 1/4 inches are in 3.5 inches.
Step 2: Convert 3.5 to a fraction or decimal 3.5 = 3.5.
Step 3: Divide 3.5 by 0.25 (which is 1/4: 3.5 \ 0.25 = 14.
Step 4: Since each unit represents 1 foot, the answer is 14 feet.

13. Correct Answer: C (480)
Step 1: Calculate the rate per hour: $150 (parts) \ 2.5 (hours) = 60 parts/hour.
Step 2: Multiply the hourly rate by the new time:
60 X 8 = 480 parts.

14. Correct Answer: C (76 inches)
Step 1: Convert feet to inches: 6 (feet) X 12 (inches) = 72 inches.
Step 2: Add the remaining inches: 72 + 4 = 76 inches.

15. Correct Answer: B (3,500 mm)
Step 1: Know the conversion: 1 {meter} = 1,000 (millimeters).
Step 2: Multiply meters by 1,000: 3.5 X 1,000 = 3,500.

16. Correct Answer: B (18.9 liters)
Step 1: Use the conversion factor provided:
1 (gal) = 3.78 (L).
Step 2: Multiply gallons by the factor: 5 X 3.78.
Step 3: 5 X 3 = 15; 5 X 0.78 = 3.9; 15 + 3.9 = 18.9.

17. Correct Answer: B (54 feet)
Step 1: Formula for perimeter of a rectangle:
P = 2 X (length) + (width).
Step 2: Add length and width: 12 + 15 = 27.
Step 3: Multiply by 2: 27 X 2 = 54.
Student Pitfall: Calculating area (12 X 15 = 180) instead of perimeter.

18. Correct Answer: C (40 sq inches)
Step 1: Formula for area of a triangle:
Area = (base X height /2.
Step 2: Multiply base and height: 10 X 8 = 80.
Step 3: Divide by 2: 80 \ 2 = 40.
Student Pitfall: Forgetting to divide by 2, leading to answer A (80).

19. Correct Answer: B (282.6 cubic feet)
Step 1: Formula for volume of a cylinder:
V = pi X r² **X** h.
Step 2: Square the radius (r=3): 3 X 3 = 9.
Step 3: Multiply by height (h=10): 9 X 10 = 90.
Step 4: Multiply by pi (3.14): 90 X 3.14 = 282.6.

20. Correct Answer: A (10 cm)
Step 1: Use the Pythagorean theorem: a² + b² = c².
Step 2: Square the legs: 6² = 36 and 8² = 64.
Step 3: Add them together: 36 + 64 = 100.
Step 4: Find the square root of 100: √100 = 10.

Science

1. A
Precision, which refers to the repeatability of measurement, does not require knowledge of the correct or true value.

2. B
A periodic table is a tabular display of the chemical elements, organized on the basis of their atomic numbers, electron configurations, and recurring chemical properties.

3. A
In terms of the scientific method, the term observation refers to the act of noticing or perceiving something and/or recording a fact or occurrence.

4. B
Kinetic energy is the energy of a body that results from motion while potential energy is the energy possessed by an object by virtue of its position or state, e.g., as in a compressed spring.

5. D
The scientific term experiment refers to a practical test designed with the intention that its results be relevant to a particular theory or set of theories.

6. B
Kinetic energy is the energy an object possesses due to its motion.

7. C
The interval of confidence around the measured value, such that the measured value is certain not to lie outside this stated interval, refers to the **uncertainty** of that value.

8. B
Metals expand when heated because particle motion increases.
Choice A (contraction) is the opposite.
Choice C (resistance) relates to electrical flow, not size.
Choice D (magnetic induction) is unrelated to heat effects.

9. D
Mechanical advantage = length ÷ height = 2 ÷ 0.5 = 4.

10. B
The current decreases
Ohm's Law: $I = V / R$ → increasing R reduces I.11.

11. B
3 m/s^2
$F = m \times a$ → $36 = 12a$ → $a = 3$.

12. C
Copper conducts electricity well and bends without breaking.
Choice A incorrect - it has low resistance).
Choice B is incorrect - it conducts heat well
Choice D is incorrect - copper is not magnetic

13. A

Pressure increases
According to Gas laws: in a sealed container, heating increases pressure.
Choice D only true if temperature remains constant.

14. B

Density decreases
Ice expands, making it less dense than liquid water.

15. C
MA = load ÷ effort = 200 ÷ 100 = 2.

16. C — Wood
Wood resists heat transfer.
Choices A, B, D are metals—excellent heat conductors.

17. B - Exothermic
Exothermic reactions release heat.
The opposite is an endothermic reaction absorbs heat from its surroundings, causing the temperature of the surroundings to decrease

18. B
1 m = 100 cm → 2.5 × 100 = 250.

19. C

Steel conducts heat away faster
High thermal conductivity makes steel feel colder.
Choice A incorrect: both are same temperature.
Choice B is incorrect - wood doesn't generate heat.
Choice D is partially true but not the primary principle.

20. C
Lubricants reduce friction and wear.
Choice A, water, offers poor lubrication.
Choice B, sand, increases friction (abrasive).
Choice D, paint, may protect but doesn't reduce friction.

Mechanical Systems

1. A
The wheel of a pulley turning is an example of torque. Torque, is the tendency of a force to rotate an object about an axis, fulcrum, or pivot. Just as a force is a push or a pull, a torque can be thought of as a twist to an object.

2. D
The block and tackle system composed of a system of pulleys as shown operates according the following rule:

Pulling Force=Load/(Number of supporting ropes)
Here, the number of supporting ropes is 4. So, we have
20 = Load/4
So, Load = 20 × 4 = 80 N.

Do not confuse the number of supporting ropes. The rope, which is being pulled, is not counted. Otherwise, you will obtain the wrong answer, Choice B 100 (20 × 5).

3. B
The equation of meshed gears states that the speed of rotation V (in rot/s) is inversely proportional to the number of teeth N. Mathematically,

$V_A/V_B = N_B/N_A$

From the figure, it is obvious that N_A = 20 and N_B = 28. So, we have

$14/V_B = 28/20$

$V_B = (14 \times 20)/28 = 10$ turns

4. C
In meshed gears, larger the gear, slower the rotation and vice versa. Thus, gear B rotates slower than the others and gear A rotates the fastest.

5. B
The smaller the distance between threads, the easier to turn.

6. C
75 pounds of force much be exerted downward on the rope to lift the 150 pound weight.

7. B
To solve for F, Weight X b (distance from fulcrum to weight) = Force X a (distance from fulcrum to point where force is applied)
100 X 5 = F X 10
500/10 = F
F =50

8. B
First calculate the speed of gear B. The gear ratio is 10:40 or 1:4. If gear A is turning at 80 rpm, then gear B, which is larger, will turn slower, 80/4 = 20 rpm.

Next calculate B and C. Gear C is smaller, so it will turn faster. The gear ratio is 40:10 or 4:1, and since gear B turns at 20 rpm, gear C will turn at 20 X 4 = 80 rpm.

Next calculate the direction. Gear A is turning clockwise, so Gear B is turning counter clockwise, so Gear C must be turning clockwise.

9. B
If the springs in parallel compress 10 inches, then the springs in series will expand half that amount, or 5 inches.

10. B
If the springs in parallel expand 20 inches, then the springs in series will expand twice that amount, or 10 inches.

11. C
Notice the weight is attached to two of the pulleys. The weight required will therefore be 100/4 = 25 pounds.

12. B
A cam is a rotating or sliding piece in a mechanical linkage used especially in transforming rotary motion into linear motion or vice-versa

13. A
The function of the crankshaft is to transform the back-and-forth motion of the pistons into rotary motion.

14. A
The labelled components are, 1 - ratchet, 2 - pawl, 3 - base.

15. C
Here, there are 3 fixed pulleys forming a single system. It is known that fixed pulleys do not provide any gain in force. So, we have P = F

16. A
Here we have the combination of two systems composed of an inclined plane and a movable pulley.
The equation of the inclined plane is
Load/Force=(Path distance)/Height=Mechanical advantage

So, the mechanical advantage MA of the inclined plane is
MA = 2h/h = 2
The equation of the movable pulley is
Mechanical advantage= (Load)/(Force) = 2

Therefore, the total mechanical advantage is 2 × 2 = 4. This means the force needed to lift the 200 N weight is 200N / 4 = 50N (choice A).

17. A
Here, we have a system of combined pulley, i.e. one fixed and one movable. The fixed pulley does not provide any mechanical advantage while the movable pulley provides a mechanical advantage of 2.
So, the force required to lift the 400 N weight (load) is:
F = W/2 = 400N/2 = 200N

18. D
The equation of meshed gears states that the speed of rotation V (in rot/s) is inversely proportional to the number of teeth N. Mathematically,

$N_1 \cdot V_1 = N_2 \cdot V_2 = N_3 \cdot V_3$

Here, we are concerned only for the gears 1 and 3. Thus, we have
$7 \cdot V_1 = 30 \cdot 210$
$V_1 = (30 \cdot 210)/7 = 900$ turns

19. C
This is a second-class lever as the Load is between pivot and force.

The equation of levers is
Load × Load distance = Force × Force distance
Here, Load = G = 600N, Load distance = y = 2m, Force distance = x + y = 3m + 2m = 5m and calculate the force.
So,

600 X 2 = F X 5

F = (600 X 2)/5 = 1200/5 = 240N

20. C
This is an example of first-class lever as the pivot (fulcrum) is between Load and Force.

The equation of levers is
Load × Load distance = Force × Force distance

Here, Load = 3m · g, Force = m · g, Load distance = (120 − x) cm, and Force distance = x cm. Here, we have to calculate the force distance. So,

3mg × (120 - x) = mg × x

Simplifying mg from both sides, the equation becomes,

3 × (120 - x) = x

3 × 120 − 3 × x = x

4x = 360

X = 90cm

Spatial Visualization

1. **B**
2. **D**
3. **B**
4. **B**
5. **A**
6. **A**

7. C

8. B

9. D

10. C

11. A
If two pieces have the same number at the position shown, it means that point is a junction point. Here, all the small shapes are on the rectangular platform, where the triangular shape is on left-bottom corner and the three small cubes are at the other corners of the platform.

12. B
If two pieces have the same number at the position shown, it means that point is a junction point. Here, the hoses are at the central holes of the lateral faces of the platform, the screw-like shape is on top of the platform and the small cuboids act as legs.

13. B
If two pieces have the same number at the position shown, it means that point is a junction point. Following this rule, here will find that the correct assembly is shown at A.

14. D
Block A touches 3 blocks in total: 2 are laterally placed and the other is below it.

15. A
Block B touches 5 blocks below and 2 laterally placed, i.e. in total 7 blocks.

16. B
Block C touches 1 blocks below, 5 laterally placed blocks, and 3 other blocks above it, i.e. 9 blocks in total.

17. B
A large perfect cube is formed when it has the dimensions 4 × 4 × 4.

The first row is complete, the second row has one cube missing, the third row has another cube is missing, and the fourth, upper row, 1 + 3 + 0 + 1 = 5 cubes are missing.

Hence, in total, 1 + 1 + 5 = 7 cubes are missing to form a perfect cube.

18. A
If you rotate the shapes in the choices by 90° clockwise, you will notice that the missing shape to form a perfect cube is the first one.

19. D
There are 5 missing cubes in the first row, 1 in the second and 5 in the third row. The only shape that fits the description is the fourth one. No rotation is needed.

20. B
There is one missing small square in the first row, one in the second and four squares in the third row. The only shape that fits the description is the second one. It does not need any rotation.

THE FINAL INSPECTION

Ready to Test Your Skills? Below you will find a full-length practice test. Please note that these are not the exact questions from the official exam—those are kept secret and change every year. Instead, we have created questions that mirror the style and difficulty of the official test.

The Bottom Line: If you can answer these questions correctly, you have the knowledge needed to pass the real exam.

Instructions:

Get in the Zone: Set aside uninterrupted time in a quiet room.

Focus: Read the instructions and every question carefully. Answer to the best of your ability.

Simulate: Use the provided bubble answer sheets to mimic the real test experience.

Review: Once finished, check your work against the Answer Key and read the explanations for any questions you missed.

Pro Tip: Do not attempt more than one practice test in a single day. Rest is just as important as practice. Wait 48 to 72 hours between tests for maximum retention.

Interpreting Written Material

	A	B	C	D	E		A	B	C	D	E
1	○	○	○	○	○	21	○	○	○	○	○
2	○	○	○	○	○	22	○	○	○	○	○
3	○	○	○	○	○	23	○	○	○	○	○
4	○	○	○	○	○	24	○	○	○	○	○
5	○	○	○	○	○	25	○	○	○	○	○
6	○	○	○	○	○						
7	○	○	○	○	○						
8	○	○	○	○	○						
9	○	○	○	○	○						
10	○	○	○	○	○						
11	○	○	○	○	○						
12	○	○	○	○	○						
13	○	○	○	○	○						
14	○	○	○	○	○						
15	○	○	○	○	○						
16	○	○	○	○	○						
17	○	○	○	○	○						
18	○	○	○	○	○						
19	○	○	○	○	○						
20	○	○	○	○	○						

Toolbox Math

	A	B	C	D	E			A	B	C	D	E
1	○	○	○	○	○		21	○	○	○	○	○
2	○	○	○	○	○		22	○	○	○	○	○
3	○	○	○	○	○		23	○	○	○	○	○
4	○	○	○	○	○		24	○	○	○	○	○
5	○	○	○	○	○		25	○	○	○	○	○
6	○	○	○	○	○							
7	○	○	○	○	○							
8	○	○	○	○	○							
9	○	○	○	○	○							
10	○	○	○	○	○							
11	○	○	○	○	○							
12	○	○	○	○	○							
13	○	○	○	○	○							
14	○	○	○	○	○							
15	○	○	○	○	○							
16	○	○	○	○	○							
17	○	○	○	○	○							
18	○	○	○	○	○							
19	○	○	○	○	○							
20	○	○	○	○	○							

Science

	A	B	C	D
1	○	○	○	○
2	○	○	○	○
3	○	○	○	○
4	○	○	○	○
5	○	○	○	○
6	○	○	○	○
7	○	○	○	○
8	○	○	○	○
9	○	○	○	○
10	○	○	○	○
11	○	○	○	○
12	○	○	○	○
13	○	○	○	○
14	○	○	○	○
15	○	○	○	○
16	○	○	○	○
17	○	○	○	○
18	○	○	○	○
19	○	○	○	○
20	○	○	○	○

Mechanical Systems

	A	B	C	D
1	○	○	○	○
2	○	○	○	○
3	○	○	○	○
4	○	○	○	○
5	○	○	○	○
6	○	○	○	○
7	○	○	○	○
8	○	○	○	○
9	○	○	○	○
10	○	○	○	○
11	○	○	○	○
12	○	○	○	○
13	○	○	○	○
14	○	○	○	○
15	○	○	○	○
16	○	○	○	○
17	○	○	○	○
18	○	○	○	○
19	○	○	○	○
20	○	○	○	○

Spatial Visualization

	A	B	C	D
1	○	○	○	○
2	○	○	○	○
3	○	○	○	○
4	○	○	○	○
5	○	○	○	○
6	○	○	○	○
7	○	○	○	○
8	○	○	○	○
9	○	○	○	○
10	○	○	○	○
11	○	○	○	○
12	○	○	○	○
13	○	○	○	○
14	○	○	○	○
15	○	○	○	○
16	○	○	○	○
17	○	○	○	○
18	○	○	○	○
19	○	○	○	○
20	○	○	○	○

Interpreting Written Material

Questions 1 - 4 refer to the following passage.

Instruction Manual Excerpt: Portable Cement Mixer

Operating Instructions:

Place the mixer on stable, level ground before adding materials.

Connect the mixer to a grounded electrical outlet.

Add gravel and sand before adding water. Cement powder should be added last.

Do not exceed the maximum fill line marked inside the drum.

Allow the drum to rotate for 3–5 minutes before pouring.

Shut off power and clean the drum immediately after use to prevent hardened buildup.

1. According to the instructions, what must be done first before operating the cement mixer?

    a. Add gravel and sand to the drum

    b. Place the mixer on stable, level ground

    c. Connect the mixer to an extension cord

    d. Add water to test rotation

2. In what order should materials be added?

    a. Water → cement → gravel

    b. Cement → sand → water

    c. Gravel and sand → water → cement

    d. Cement → water → sand

3. Why must the drum be cleaned immediately after use?

    a. To avoid contaminating the next batch of cement

    b. To prevent hardened material from building up

    c. To reduce electrical strain on the motor

    d. To ensure accurate measurement of sand

4. What could happen if the maximum fill line is exceeded?

    a. The drum may not rotate properly

    b. The cement will dry faster

    c. The mixer will automatically shut off

    d. The materials will lose their bonding strength

Questions 5 - 8 refer to the following passage.

ABC Electric Warranty

ABC Electric Company warrants that its products are free from defects in material and workmanship. Subject to the conditions and limitations set forth below, ABC Electric will, at its option, either repair or replace any part of its products that prove defective due to improper workmanship or materials.

This limited warranty does not cover any damage to the product from improper installation, accident, abuse, misuse, natural disaster, insufficient or excessive electrical supply, abnormal mechanical or environmental conditions, or any unauthorized disassembly, repair, or modification.

This limited warranty also does not apply to any product on which the original identification information has been altered, or removed, has not been handled or packaged correctly, or has been sold as second-hand.

This limited warranty covers only repair, replacement, refund or credit for defective ABC Electric products, as provided above.

5. I tried to repair my ABC Electric blender, but could not, so can I get it repaired under this warranty?

    a. Yes, the warranty still covers the blender

    b. No, the warranty does not cover the blender

    c. Uncertain. ABC Electric may or may not cover repairs under this warranty

6. My ABC Electric fan is not working. Will ABC Electric provide a new one or repair this one?

    a. ABC Electric will repair my fan

    b. ABC Electric will replace my fan

    c. ABC Electric could either replace or repair my fan can request either a replacement or a repair.

7. My stove was damaged in a flood. Does this warranty cover my stove?

    a. Yes, it is covered.

    b. No, it is not covered.

    c. It may or may not be covered.

    d. ABC Electric will decide if it is covered

8. Which of the following is an example of improper workmanship?

   a. Missing parts
   b. Defective parts
   c. Scratches on the front
   d. None of the above

Tool Manual Warning Label

Always disconnect the drill from power before changing bits. Failure to do so may cause accidental activation, resulting in injury."

9. What is the main purpose of this warning?

   a. To prevent overheating of the drill
   b. To avoid accidental activation during bit changes
   c. To reduce electricity usage
   d. To ensure the drill stays clean

Construction Site Note

"The south staircase will be closed from 10 a.m. to 2 p.m. for concrete curing. Use the temporary access ramp on the east side."

10. What should workers do between 10 a.m. and 2 p.m.?

    a. Use the east-side access ramp
    b. Use the south staircase only
    c. Pour additional concrete
    d. Avoid entering the building

MSDS Excerpt

"Avoid inhaling vapours. Prolonged exposure may cause headaches or nausea. Use in well-ventilated areas."

11. What is the recommended preventive measure?

    a. Wear steel-toe boots

    b. Work outdoors or with ventilation

    c. Use water to dilute vapour

    d. Store in warm areas

Questions 13 - 16 refer to the following passage.

LOCKOUT/TAGOUT INSTRUCTIONS

Before repairing or cleaning a piece of electrical equipment, workers must follow the company's Lockout/Tagout (LOTO) procedure. First, the technician must switch off the main power and secure it with a personal lock. A red "DO NOT OPERATE" tag must be attached with the worker's name, department, and the date. After locking out the power, the technician must test the equipment to confirm it cannot start. Only the worker who applied the lock and tag is permitted to remove them once the job is complete.

12. What is the primary purpose of the Lockout/Tagout procedure?

    a. To record who is working in a specific department

    b. To prevent equipment from being used outside of business hours

    c. To ensure equipment cannot be energized during maintenance

    d. To speed up repair and cleaning tasks

13. According to the procedure, what must be done immediately after switching off the main power?

   a. Test the equipment
   b. Remove the safety tag
   c. Apply a personal lock and tag
   d. Inform the supervisor

14. What information must be included on the tag?

   a. The worker's lunch break schedule
   b. Name, department, and date
   c. Supervisor's signature
   d. Length of the repair

15. Who is permitted to remove the lock and tag?

   a. Any trained technician
   b. The shift supervisor
   c. The worker who applied them
   d. The safety coordinator

Instruction Manual (Electrical)

Before installing the new ceiling fan model #CF-700, ensure the main breaker to the circuit is in the OFF position. Attach the mounting bracket to the junction box using two 1/2-inch wood screws. The bracket must be able to support a minimum of 50 pounds. Connect the green ground wire from the bracket to the bare copper wire in the junction box. Next, connect the white neutral wires and the black hot wires, securing each connection with a wire nut and a wrap of electrical tape. Failure to correctly attach the ground wire could result in an electrical shock hazard. The fan blades should be attached after the motor housing is securely fastened to the mounting bracket.

16. According to the passage, what is the first step a technician must take before beginning the installation?

    a. Attach the fan blades.

    b. Connect the wires.

    c. Turn the main breaker to the OFF position.

    d. Secure the motor housing.

17. Which pair of wires must be connected to ensure the fan is properly grounded?

    a. The black wire and the white wire.

    b. The green wire and the bare copper wire.

    c. The 1/2-inch wood screws.

    d. The wire nut and electrical tape.

18. How much weight must the mounting bracket be capable of supporting?

    a. Exactly 1/2-inch.

    b. More than 700 pounds.

    c. A minimum of 50 pounds.

    d. Up to two wood screws.

19. What is the potential hazard mentioned if the ground wire is not correctly attached?

    a. The fan will spin too fast.

    b. The wire nut will fall off.

    c. An electrical shock hazard.

    d. The mounting bracket will fail.

Safety Data Sheet (SDS) - Section 7 (Welding Flux)

SDS Section 7: Handling and Storage

Precautions for Safe Handling: Avoid breathing dust/fume/gas/mist/vapors/spray. Do not eat, drink, or smoke when using this product. Use only outdoors or in a well-ventilated area. Always wear appropriate Personal Protective Equipment (PPE), including safety glasses and leather welding gloves. Wash thoroughly after handling.

Conditions for Safe Storage, including any Incompatibilities: Store in a dry, cool, and well-ventilated place. Keep container tightly closed when not in use. Store away from oxidizing agents and strong acids. Keep out of reach of children.

The recommended maximum storage temperature is 25^0 (77^0F).

20. What temperature is the recommended maximum for storing this welding flux?

    a. Exactly 77^0 F

    b. 25^0 C or 77^0 F

    c. Above 25^0 C

    d. A dry, cool temperature.

21. What necessary action is specified to be done after handling the product?

    a. Store it away from strong acids.

    b. Keep the container tightly closed.

    c. Wash thoroughly.

    d. Put on safety glasses and gloves.

22. Which of the following conditions is incompatible with the safe storage of the welding flux?

    a. A dry and cool place.

    b. Storing away from strong acids.

    c. Storage near an oxidizing agent.

    d. Keeping the container tightly closed.

23. If a welder is working indoors with this product, what is the required condition for the work area?

    a. It must be $25°$ (C).

    b. Eating and drinking are permitted.

    c. It must be a well-ventilated area.

    d. Welding gloves are optional

Toolbox Math

Part 1: Applied Arithmetic & Estimation

1. A plumber charges a flat fee of $60 for a service call plus $45 per hour of labor. If a job takes 3 hours, what is the total bill?

    a. 135
    b. 180
    c. 195
    d. 315

2. A box of 500 screws costs 25. What is the unit price per screw?

    a. 0.05
    b. 0.50
    c. 0.02
    d. 0.20

3. Evaluate: 100 - 24 \ (2 X 3).

    a. 12.6
    b. 96
    c. 38
    d. 4

Part 2: Fractions in the Trades

4. A mechanic uses a 5/8-inch wrench, but it is slightly too small. Which size is the next size larger in standard 1/16 increments?

    a. 11/16} inch
    b. 3/4 inch
    c. 9/16 inch
    d. 1/2 inch

5. A board is 96 inches long. If you cut it into 5 equal pieces (ignoring saw kerf), how long is each piece expressed as a mixed number?

    a. 19 1/5 inches
    b. 19 1/4 inches
    c. 18 3/4 inches
    d. 19 1/2 inches

6. What is 7/8 - 1/4?

    a. 6/4
    b. 3/8
    c. 5/8
    d. 1/2

Part 3: Decimals & Tolerance

7. A machinist measures a part as 2.504 inches. The blueprint requires 2.500 ± 0.005. Is the part within tolerance?

    a. No, it is too small.
    b. No, it is too large.
    c. Yes, it is within tolerance.
    d. Cannot be determined.

8. Convert 0.625 to a fraction in lowest terms.

    a. 5/8
    b. 3/5
    c. 3/8
    d. 2/3

9. Three resistors have values of 12.5 ohms, 4.25 ohms, and 100.1 ohms. What is the total resistance when added in series?

    a. 116.85 ohms
    b. 116.35 ohms
    c. 117.85 ohms
    d. 157.1 ohms

Part 4: Percentages & Material Waste

10. You need to tile a 200 sq. ft. floor. You should purchase 10% extra for breakage and waste. How many total square feet of tile should you buy?

    a. 210 sq. ft.
    b. 202 sq. ft.
    c. 220 sq. ft.
    d. 250 sq. ft.

11. A tool is on sale for 20% off. If the original price was 80, what is the sale price?

    a. $16
    b. $60
    c. $64
    d. $72

Part 5: Measurement Conversion

12. An HVAC technician measures a duct as 54 inches long. What is this length in feet and inches?

    a. 5 feet 4 inches
    b. 4 feet 6 inches
    c. 4 feet 8 inches
    d. 3 feet 10 inches

13. How many ounces are in 2.5 pounds? (1 pound = 16 ounces)

    a. 32 oz
    b. 36 oz
    c. 40 oz
    d. 25 oz

14. A road is 2 kilometers long. How many meters is this?

    a. 200 m

    b. 2,000 m

    c. 20,000 m

    d. 20 m

Part 6: Geometry (Area, Volume, Angles)

15. Find the area of a circle with a radius of 4 inches. (Use pi approx 3.14)

    a. 12.56 sq inches

    b. 25.12 sq inches

    c. 50.24 sq inches

    d. 16 sq inches

16. What is the area of the L-shaped floor shown below? (A rectangle 10 X 10 with a 5 X 5 corner remove

    a. 100 sq ft

    b. 50 sq ft

    c. 75 sq ft

    d. 85 sq ft

17. Concrete is ordered in cubic yards. You need to fill a volume of 54 cubic feet. How many cubic yards is this? (1 cubic yard = 27 cubic feet)

    a. 1.5 cubic yards

    b. 2 cubic yards

    c. 3 cubic yards

    d. 0.5 cubic yards

18. In a right triangle, one acute angle measures 35°. What is the measure of the other acute angle?

    a. 145°
    b. 65°
    c. 55°
    d. 45°

19. A ladder is placed against a wall. The base is 5 feet from the wall, and the ladder reaches 12 feet up the wall. What is the length of the ladder?

    a. 13 feet
    b. 17 feet
    c. 15 feet
    d. 12.5 feet

20. A room has a volume of 1,200 cubic feet. If the floor area is 150 square feet, what is the height of the ceiling?

    a. 10 feet
    b. 8 feet
    c. 12 feet
    d. 9 feet

Science

1. Electrons play a critical role in:

    a. Electricity
    b. Magnetism
    c. Thermal conductivity
    d. All of the above

2. An idea concerning a phenomena and possible explanations for that phenomena is a/an

   a. Theory
   b. Experiment
   c. Inference
   d. Hypothesis

3. What is the earth's primary source of energy?

   a. Water
   b. The sun
   c. Electromagnetic radiation
   d. Weak nuclear force

4. What type of research is to determine the relationship between one thing (an independent variable) and another (a dependent or outcome variable) in a population.

   a. Qualitative
   b. Quantitative
   c. Independent
   d. Scientific

5. What can accept a hydrogen ion and can react with fats to form soap?

   a. Acid
   b. Salt
   c. Base
   d. Foundation

6. **How many elements are represented on the periodic table?**

    a. 122 elements

    b. 99 elements

    c. 102 elements

    d. 118 elements

7. **What is the process of converting observed phenomena into data is called?**

    a. Calculation

    b. Measurement

    c. Valuation

    d. Estimation

8. **The mass number of an atom is:**

    a. The total number of particles that make it up

    b. The total weight of an atom

    c. The total mass of an atom

    d. None of the above

9. **What is sublimation?**

    a. A phase transition from liquid to gas

    b. A phase transition from solid to gas

    c. A phase transition from gas to liquid

    d. A phase transition from gas to solid

10. **A practical test designed with the intention that its results will be relevant to a particular theory or set of theories is a/an**

    a. Experiment

    b. Practicum

    c. Theory

    d. Design

11. A worker needs to lift a heavy crate. They use a long steel bar pivoting on a rock (a fulcrum) to lift it. To make lifting the crate easier (requiring less force), where should the fulcrum be placed?

    a. Exactly in the middle of the bar.

    b. As close to the crate (load) as possible.

    c. As close to the worker's hands (effort) as possible.

    d. Placement does not change the force required.

12. You are using a block and tackle pulley system with 4 sections of rope supporting the load. If the load weighs 100 lbs, approximately how much force do you need to pull on the rope to lift it? (Ignore friction and rope weight).

    a. 400 lbs

    b. 100 lbs

    c. 50 lbs

    d. 25 lbs

13. In a hydraulic lift system, a small piston pushes down on the fluid, lifting a large piston. According to Pascal's Law, how does the pressure at the small piston compare to the pressure at the large piston?

    a. The pressure is significantly higher at the small piston.

    b. The pressure is significantly higher at the large piston.

    c. The pressure is equal at both pistons.

    d. The pressure depends on the viscosity of the oil.

14. An electric heater is rated at 1500 Watts. "Watts" is a unit measuring:

    a. Electrical Resistance

    b. Electrical Pressure

    c. Power (Energy usage rate)

    d. Current flow

15. Why are gaps intentionally left between sections of railway tracks or concrete bridges?

    a. To save money on materials.

    b. To allow for drainage of rainwater.

    c. To allow for thermal expansion during hot weather.

    d. To increase the friction for trains or cars.

16. Heat is traveling through a solid copper pipe from the hot end to the cold end. This method of heat transfer is known as:

    a. Convection

    b. Radiation

    c. Conduction

    d. Insulation

17. Why is "galvanized" steel coated with a layer of zinc?

    a. To make the steel stronger and harder.

    b. To allow the steel to conduct electricity better.

    c. To prevent the steel from rusting (corrosion).

    d. To make the steel lighter.

18. Which components are required to sustain a fire (The Fire Triangle)?

    a. Fuel, Oxygen, and Heat.

    b. Fuel, Nitrogen, and Water.

    c. Spark, Wind, and Wood.

    d. Carbon Dioxide, Heat, and Fuel.

19. What is the primary function of a fuse or circuit breaker?

    a. To increase the voltage if it drops too low.

    b. To interrupt the circuit if the current becomes too high (overload).

    c. To store electricity for later use.

    d. To convert AC power to DC power.

20. Two gears are meshed together. Gear A (the driver) has 10 teeth. Gear B (the driven) has 20 teeth. If Gear A turns at 100 RPM, how fast will Gear B turn?

    a. 200 RPM

    b. 100 RPM

    c. 50 RPM

    d. 20 RPM

Mechanical Systems

1. What is the value of the force F enough to lift the object up, if the weight W of the object is 360 N?

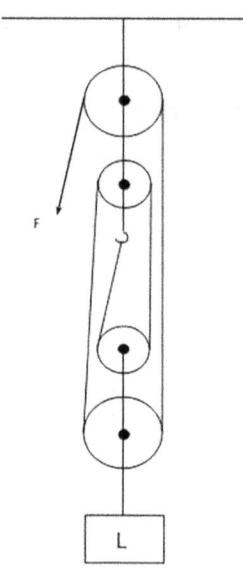

    a. 180 N

    b. 120 N

    c. 90 N

    d. 72 N

2. How many turns does the gear A make if the gear B makes 100 turns?

    a. 175

    b. 70

    c. 7

    d. 5

3. Which of the following statements about gears is false?

   a. Gears are teethed wheels used to generate rotation
   b. Meshed gears move at the same time
   c. Meshed gears move at the same speed
   d. Teeth in gears help increase the friction and avoid slipping

4. What direction does the rack in the figure move if the pinion rotates clockwise?

   a. Left
   b. Right
   c. Up
   d. Down

5. What direction does the pinion in the figure rotate if the rack shifts on the right?

   a. Clockwise
   b. Counter-clockwise
   c. First clockwise then counter-clockwise
   d. First counter-clockwise, then clockwise

6. The system shown is in equilibrium and the rod is weightless. What is the ratio P/F ?

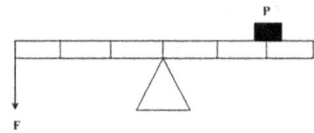

a. 3/2
b. 2/3
c. 1
d. 5/3

7. What is the ratio of the load to effort?

a. Torque
b. Mechanical Advantage
c. Energy
d. Mechanical Energy

8. Which type of lever does the wheel and axle system shown represent?

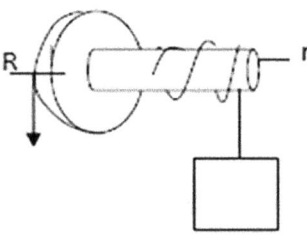

a. First class lever
b. Second class lever
c. Third class lever
d. Fourth class lever

9. **What is the working principle of sugar tongs?**

   a. First class lever
   b. Second class lever
   c. Third class lever
   d. Fourth class lever

10. **Find the value of the ratio F/W, if R/r = 3.**

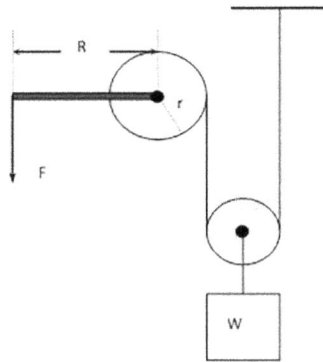

   a. 3
   b. 1/3
   c. 6
   d. 1/6

11. In the figure above m_1 = 4 kg and m_2 = 2 kg. What is the value of m_3 in kg if the system is in equilibrium? (The rod is weightless)

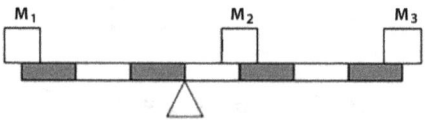

a. 2
b. 2.5
c. 3
d. 3.5

12. What is the reading of dynamo-meter in the figure below if the system is in equilibrium? The bar has no mass.

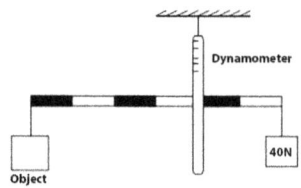

a. 20N
b. 40N
c. 60N
d. 80N

13. A uniform rod can be hold in equilibrium with the help of a system of pulleys as in the figure below. What is the weight of the rod if the force F = 3N?

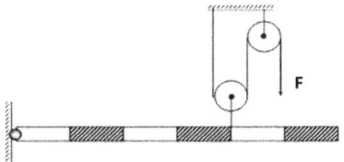

a. 3N
b. 4N
c. 6N
d. 8N

14. The length of the lever is 1 meter. What is the mechanical advantage of the system?

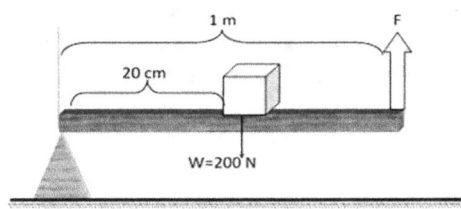

a. 1/5
b. 5
c. 1/2
d. 2

15. What is the effort-distance for the system shown?

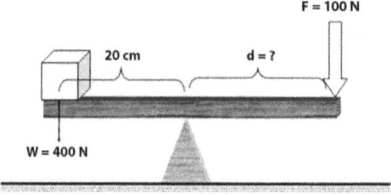

  a. 5 cm
  b. 40 cm
  c. 80 cm
  d. 100 cm

16. A door handle is an example of

  a. Inclined plane
  b. Pulley
  c. Screw
  d. Lever

17. The values of the acting force and the load are F = 20 N and P = 100 N respectively for the system shown. The total length of the lever rod is 120 cm. What is the distance between the force and the fulcrum (support) in cm?

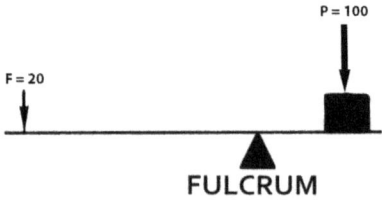

a. 70
b. 80
c. 90
d. 100

Spatial Visualization

1. When folded, what pattern is possible?

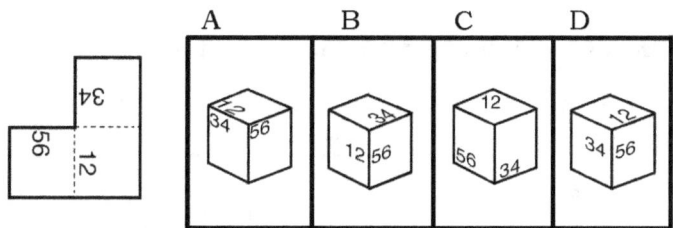

2. When folded into a loop, what will the strip of paper look like?

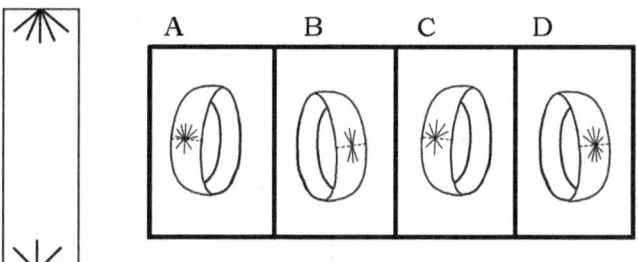

3. Which of the choices is the same pattern at a different angle?

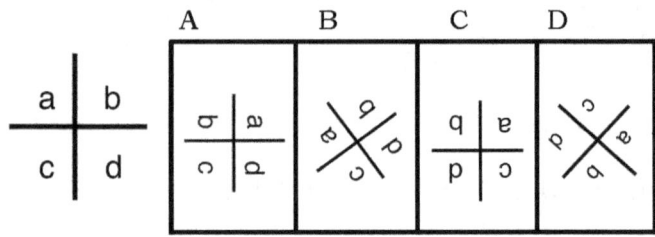

4. When folded, what pattern is possible?

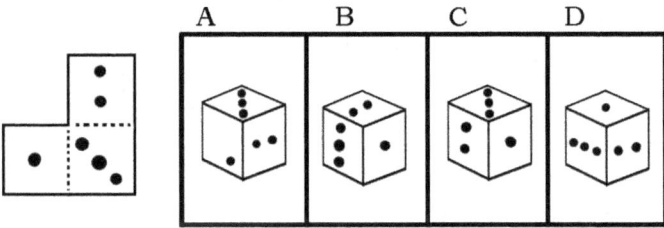

5. Which of the choices is the same pattern at a different angle?

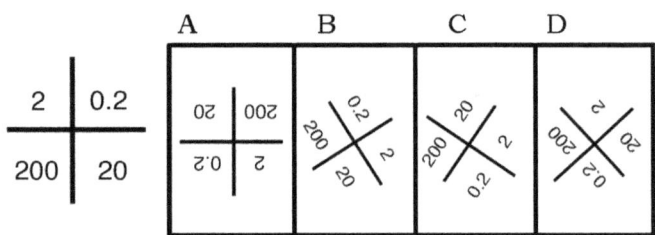

6. When folded along the dotted lines, which shape will you get?

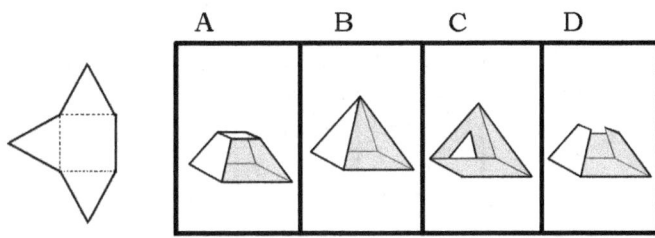

7. When folded, what pattern is possible?

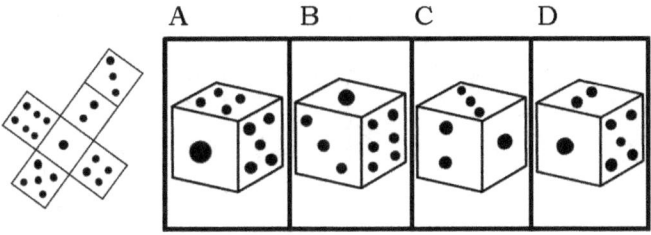

8. When folded into a loop, what will the strip of paper look like?

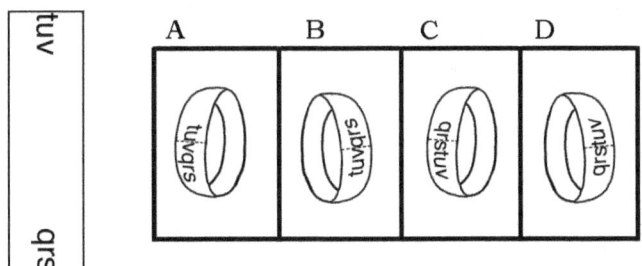

9. Which of the choices is the same pattern at a different angle?

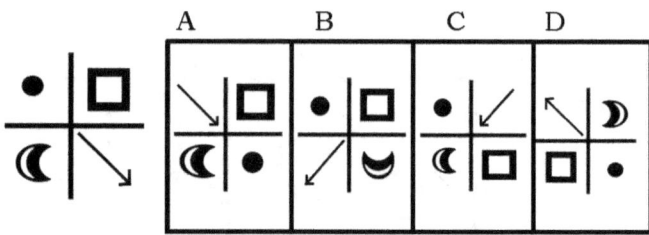

10. When put together, what 3-dimensional shape will you get?

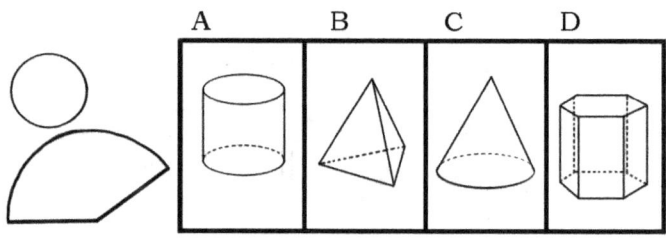

11. Which figure represents the assembly of the following pieces?

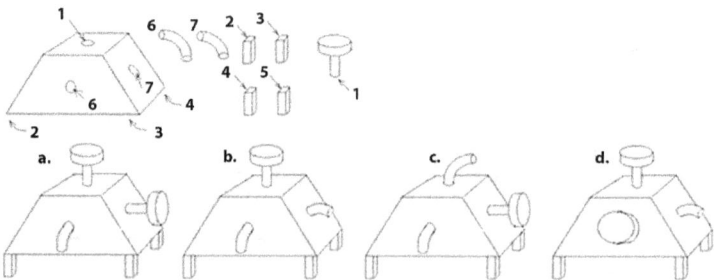

12. Which figure represents the assembly of the following pieces?

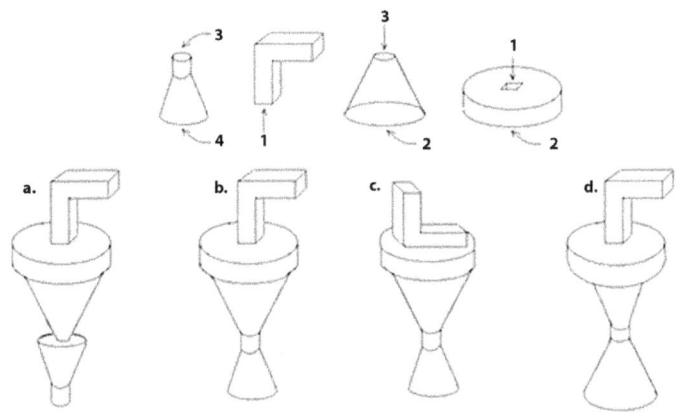

13. Which figure represents the assembly of the following pieces?

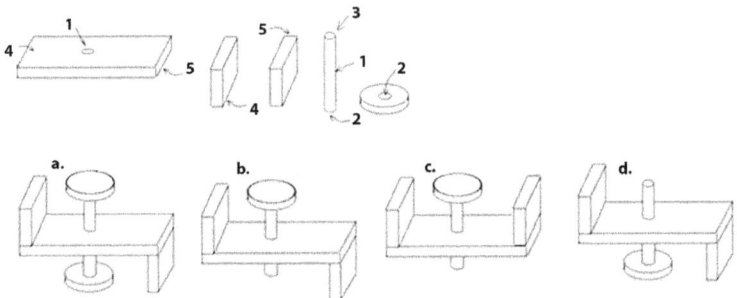

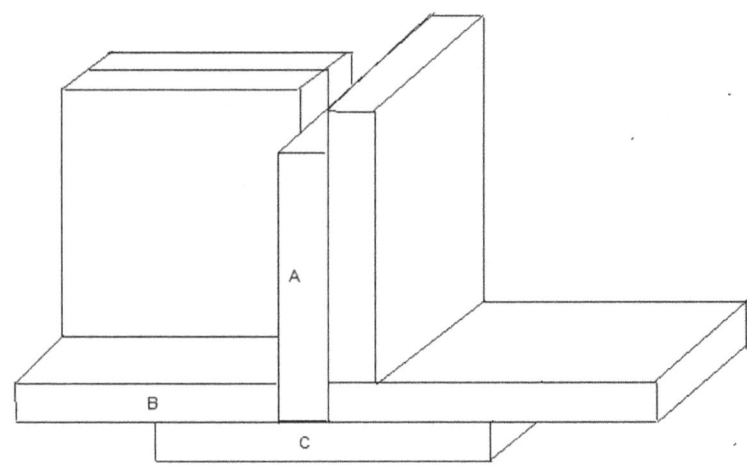

14. How many blocks is block A touching?

    a. 7
    b. 6
    c. 5
    d. 4

15. How many blocks is block B touching?

    a. 4
    b. 5
    c. 6
    d. 3

16. How many blocks is block C touching?

    a. 4
    b. 3
    c. 2
    d. 1

17. How many cubes must we add in the figure to form a perfect cube?

a. 55
b. 45
c. 70
d. 125

18. Which shape must we place to the right side of the figure to balance the weight of the system? All shapes are made by the same material.

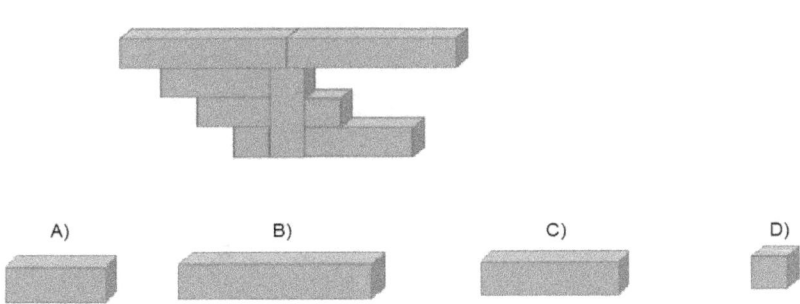

A)   B)   C)   D)

19. Which shape must we place on the existing figure to form a perfect square?

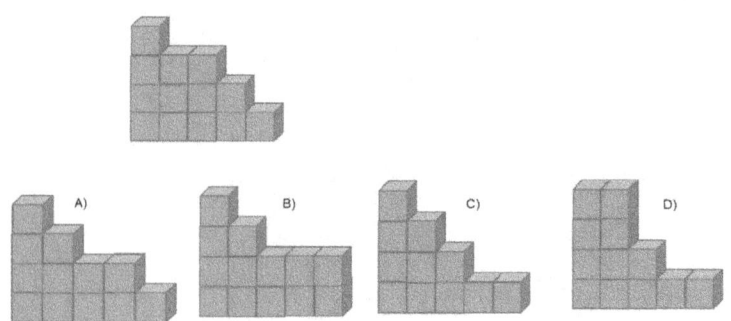

20. How many small cubes are missing in the figure to form a large perfect cube?

    a. 6
    b. 7
    c. 8
    d. 9

Answer Key

1. B
Step 1: place mixer on stable, level ground.

2. C
Gravel/sand first → water → cement powder last.

3. B
Cleaning prevents hardened buildup.

4. A
Overfilling can cause poor rotation or mechanical strain.

5. B
This warranty does not cover a product that you have tried to fix yourself. From paragraph two, "This limited warranty does not cover ... any unauthorized disassembly, repair, or modification. "

6. C
ABC Electric could either replace or repair the fan, provided the other conditions are met. ABC Electric has the option to repair or replace.

7. B
The warranty does not cover a stove damaged in a flood. From the passage, "This limited warranty does not cover any damage to the product from improper installation, accident, abuse, misuse, natural disaster, insufficient or excessive electrical supply, abnormal mechanical or environmental conditions."

A flood is an "abnormal environmental condition," and a natural disaster, so it is not covered.

8. A
A missing part is an example of defective workmanship. This is an error made in the manufacturing process. A defective part is not considered workmanship.

9. B
Preventing accidental activation reduces injury risk.

10. A
Instruction clearly directs workers to the ramp.

11. B
Ventilation reduces vapour concentration.

12. B
The passage states, The recommended maximum storage temperature is $25°$ C or $77°$ F.

13. C
The instructions for safe handling conclude with the instruction, "Wash thoroughly after handling."

14. C
The storage conditions list storing "away from oxidizing agents and strong acids." Storing near them is an incompatibility.

15. C
The safety precaution advises to "Use only outdoors or in a well-ventilated area," and this applies to indoor use as well.

16. C
The passage states, "Before installing... ensure the main breaker... is in the OFF position." This is the mandatory first step.

17. B
The passage says to "Connect the green ground wire from the bracket to the bare copper wire in the junction box."

18. C
The passage specifies, "The bracket must be able to support a minimum of 50 pounds."

19. C
The text explicitly warns, "Failure to correctly attach the ground wire could result in an electrical shock hazard."

20. B
The passage states, "The recommended maximum storage temperature is 250 (770 F)."

21. C
The instructions for safe handling conclude with the instruction, "Wash thoroughly after handling."

22. C
The storage conditions list storing "away from oxidizing agents and strong acids." Storing near them is an incompatibility.

23. C
The safety precaution advises to "Use only outdoors or in a well-ventilated area," and this applies to indoor use as well.

Toolbox Math

1. Correct Answer: C ($195)
Step 1: Calculate labor cost: 3 (hours) X 45 = 135.
Step 2: Add the flat fee: 135 + 60 = $195.

Student Pitfall: Adding the flat fee to the hourly rate first (60 + 45) and then multiplying by 3, resulting in $315.

2. Correct Answer: A ($0.05)
Step 1: Set up division: (Total Cost) \ (Quantity).
Step 2: 25 \ 500 = 0.05.
Student Pitfall: Dividing 500 by 25 (=20), leading to choice D.

3. Correct Answer: B (96)
Step 1: BEDMAS/PEMDAS - Brackets first: (2 X 3) = 6.
Step 2: Division next: 24 \ 6 = 4.
Step 3: Subtraction last: 100 - 4 = 96.
Student Pitfall: Performing operations left-to-right ignoring order. 100-24=76, then divide by 6.

4. Correct Answer: A 11/16
Step 1: Convert 5/8 to sixteenths to compare: (2 X 5) \ (2 X 8) = 10/16.
Step 2: The next increment up is (10 + 1) / 16 = 11/16.
Student Pitfall: Thinking 3/4 (which is 12/16) is the next size, skipping 11/16.

5. Correct Answer: A (19 1/5)
Step 1: Divide 96 by 5. 5 goes into 90 eighteen times, with 6 left over. 5 goes into 95 nineteen times (19 X 5 = 95).
Step 2: Remainder is 1.
Step 3: Write as a mixed number: 19 1/5.

6. Correct Answer: C (5/8)
Step 1: Find Common Denominator (8). Convert 1/4 to eighths: (1 X 2) / (4 X 2} = 2/8.
Step 2: Subtract numerators: 7/8 - 2/8 = 5/8.

7. Correct Answer: C (Yes, it is within tolerance)
Step 1: Calculate the Upper Limit: 2.500 + 0.005 = 2.505.
Step 2: Calculate the Lower Limit: 2.500 - 0.005 = 2.495.
Step 3: Compare measurement (2.504). It is between 2.495 and 2.505.

8. Correct Answer: A (5/8)
Step 1: Recognize 0.625 as a common fraction. If unknown, write as 625/1000.
Step 2: Divide numerator and denominator by 125.
Step 3: 625 \ 125 = 5; 1000 \ 125 = 8. Result: 5/8.

9. Correct Answer: A (116.85 ohms)
Step 1: Line up the decimal points:
   12.50
   + 4.25
+100.10
Step 2: Sum: 116.85.
Student Pitfall: Mis-aligning decimals (e.g., adding 100.1 as if it were 10.01).

10. Correct Answer: C (220 sq. ft.)
Step 1: Calculate 10% of 200: 200 X 0.10 = 20.
Step 2: Add waste to total: 200 + 20 = 220.

11. Correct Answer: C (64)
Step 1: Calculate discount amount: 80 X 0.20 = 16.
Step 2: Subtract discount from original price: 80 - 16 = 64.
Alternate Method: Multiply by remaining percentage (80%): 80 X 0.8 = 64.

12. Correct Answer: B (4 feet 6 inches)
Step 1: Divide inches by 12: 54 \ 12.
Step 2: 12 X 4 = 48. So, there are 4 whole feet.
Step 3: Remainder: 54 - 48 = 6 inches.

13. Correct Answer: C (40 oz)
Step 1: Multiply pounds by conversion factor (16).
Step 2: 2 X 16 = 32.
Step 3: 0.5 X 16 = 8.
Step 4: 32 + 8 = 40.

14. Correct Answer: B (2,000 m)
Step 1: Metric prefix "kilo" means 1,000.
Step 2: 2 X 1,000 = 2,000.

15. Correct Answer: C (50.24 sq inches)
Step 1: Formula: Area = pi X r^2.
Step 2: Square the radius: 4 X 4 = 16.
Step 3: Multiply by pi: 16 X 3.14 = 50.24.
Student Pitfall: Calculating circumference (2 X pi X r) leading to 25.12, or multiplying pi X 4 leading to 12.56.

16. Correct Answer: C (75 sq ft)
Step 1: Calculate area of the full square as if it were complete: 10 X 10 = 100.
Step 2: Calculate area of the missing corner: 5 X 5 = 25.
Step 3: Subtract the missing piece: 100 - 25 = 75.

17. Correct Answer: B (2 cubic yards)
Step 1: Know the conversion: 27 { cu ft} = 1 (cu yd).
Step 2: Divide volume by 27: 54 \ 27 = 2.

18. Correct Answer: C (55º)
Step 1: The sum of angles in a triangle is 180º.
Step 2: A right triangle has one 90º angle.
Step 3: 180 - 90 - 35 = 55. (Or simply, acute angles in a right triangle sum to 90: 90 - 35 = 55).

19. Correct Answer: A (13 feet)

Step 1: Pythagorean Theorem: $a^2 + b^2 = c^2$.
Step 2: $5^2 + 12^2 = c^2 \rightarrow 25 + 144 = 169$.
Step 3: Square root of $\sqrt{169} = 13$.

20. Correct Answer: B (8 feet)
Step 1: Formula: Volume = Area X Height.
Step 2: Rearrange: Height = (Volume) \ (Area).
Step 3: 1200 \ 150. Drop zeros: 120 \ 15.
Step 4: Result: 8 feet.

Science

1. D
All of the above are true. Electrons play an essential role in electricity, magnetism, and thermal conductivity.

2. D
An idea concerning a phenomena and possible explanations for that phenomena is an hypothesis.

3. B
The sun is the earth's primary source of energy.

4. B
The goal of quantitative research is to determine the relationship between one thing (an independent variable) and another (a dependent or outcome variable) in a population.

5. C
A base is any substance that can accept a hydrogen ion and can react with fats to form soap.

6. D
The periodic table as it is today, contains 118 elements.

7. B
The process of converting observed phenomena into data is called Measurement.

8. A
The mass number of an atom is the total number of particles (protons and neutrons) that make it up.

9. B
Sublimation is the direct phase transition from solid to gas.

10. A
A practical test designed with the intention that its results will be relevant to a particular theory or set of theories is an experiment.

11. B
This is a Class 1 lever. To maximize Mechanical Advantage, you want the effort arm (distance from hands to fulcrum) to be long and the load arm (distance from crate to fulcrum) to be short.

Choice A provides no advantage (1:1 ratio). Choice C makes it much harder (mechanical disadvantage). Choice D is false; leverage physics dictates force requirements.

12. D
In a pulley system, the force required is roughly equal to the Weight divided by the number of supporting ropes.
100 lbs / 4 = 25 lbs.
Choice A suggests you need more force (impossible with pulleys). Choice B implies no advantage. Choice C assumes only 2 ropes.

13. C
Pascal's Law states that pressure applied to a confined fluid is transmitted undiminished throughout the fluid. $P_1 = P_2$.
The Force changes due to area, but Pressure stays constant.

Choices A and B misunderstand the difference between Force (which multiplies) and Pressure (which is constant).

14. C
Watts measure the rate of energy consumption.
Choice A is Ohms. Choice B is Volts. Choice D is Amps.

15. C
Solids expand when heated. Without a gap (expansion joint), tracks would buckle or bridges would crack on hot days.

Choices A, B, and D are not the primary engineering reason for these specific structural gaps.

16. C
Conduction is heat transfer through direct contact in solids.

Choice A (Convection) happens in fluids/gases. Choice B (Radiation) happens through space/air (like the sun). Choice D (Insulation) stops heat transfer.

17. C
Zinc acts as a sacrificial anode. It corrodes before the steel does, protecting the structural metal.

Choices A, B, and D are not the purpose of galvanization.

18. A
Fire is a chemical reaction that requires these three elements. Remove one, and the fire goes out.

Choice B includes Nitrogen (inert). Choice C misses Oxygen. Choice D includes CO_2 (which puts fires out).

19. B
It is a safety device. If current exceeds the wire's rating, it creates heat. The breaker trips to stop the fire risk.

Choice A is a transformer function. Choice C is a battery. Choice D is a rectifier/inverter.

20. C
A small gear driving a large gear reduces speed but increases torque. The ratio is 10:20 (or 1:2). The driven gear turns half as fast.
Choice A would happen if the large gear drove the small one. Choice B implies no change. Choice D is the wrong ratio.

Mechanical Systems

1. C

The block and tackle system composed of a system of pulleys as shown operates according the following rule:

Pulling Force = Load / (Number of supporting ropes)

Here Load and Weight are the same thing.

Here, the number of supporting ropes is 4. So, we have

F = 360/4

Force = 90 N Choice C

Feedback for Choice D

Do not confuse the number of supporting ropes. The rope which is being pulled is not counted. Otherwise, you will obtain the wrong answer choice D 72 (360 / 5).

2. A
The equation of meshed gears states that the speed of rotation V (in rot/s) is inversely proportional to the number of teeth N. Mathematically,
VA/VB = NB/NA

From the figure, it is obvious that NA = 20 and NB = 35. So, since the time of rotation for both gears is equal, we have

VA/100 = 35/20

VB = (100 × 35)/20 = 175 turns

3. C
Choice A is correct. Gears are teethed wheels used to generate rotation.
Choice B is correct. Meshed gears move at the same time as they are connected.
Choice C is false. Meshed gears move at different speed depending on their size. Larger gears move slower than smaller gears.
Choice D is correct. Teeth in gears help increase the friction and avoid slipping.

4. A
If the pinion rotates clockwise, its lower teeth move due left. Therefore, the rack shifts left as well.

5. B
If the rack shifts to the right, the lower part of the pinion moves right as well. This means the entire pinion rotates counter-clockwise.

6. A
The equation of levers is
Load × Load distance = Force × Force distance

Here, the load is represented by the symbol P (force is F). On the other hand, Load distance is 2 units and force distance = 3 units.

The mechanical advantage of levers is
MA = Load/Force = (Force distance)/(Load distance)

7. D
The ratio of the load to the effort is known as Mechanical Advantage (MA). It shows how many times easier it would be to perform an action using the simple machine compared to not using it. Mechanical advantage has no unit.

8. A
A lateral view of the Wheel and Axle system is shown on the right. The pivot is at the common center of the two circles. Force is on the left side and Load is on the right one. Therefore, this is an example of first class lever (Force – Pivot – Load).

9. C
Sugar tongs have their turning point at one side and the load is on the other side. We must use a force between them to catch the sugar cubes. Therefore, this is an example of third class levers (Pivot – Force – Load).

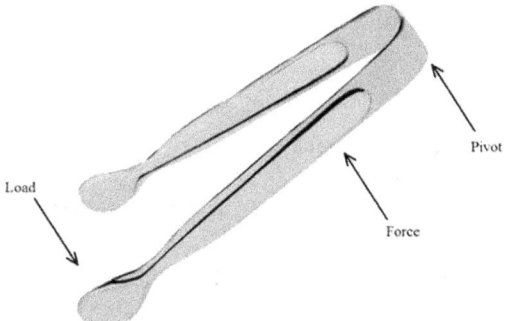

10. D
This is a combined system of simple machines composed of a Wheel and Axle and a Movable pulley system.

For the wheel and axle, the mechanical advantage is $MA_1 = R / r$. Here, MA1 = 3.

For movable pulleys, the mechanical advantage MA_2 is 2. So, the combined mechanical advantage is
$MA_{total} = MA_1 \times MA_2 = 3 \times 2 = 6$.

This means the force needed to lift the load is 6 time smaller than the load itself. So, F/W = 1/6

11. B
Since the system is in equilibrium, we have the total clockwise moment (turning effect) is equal to the counter clockwise one. The equation used in this situation is
$F_1 * d_1 = F_2 * d_2 + F_3 * d_3$

Or
$m_1 * g * d_1 = m_2 * g * d_2 + m_3 * g * d_3$
Simplifying gravity g from both sides and giving that $d_1 = 3$ units, $d_2 = 1$ unit and $d_3 = 4$ units, the equation becomes,
4 * 3 = 2 * 1 + m_3 * 4
12 = 2 + m_3 * 4
m_3 * 4 = 12 − 2 = 10
m_3 = 10/4 = 2.5 kg

12. C

First, we must find the weight of the hanging object on the left.

$W_{left} * d_{left} = W_{right} * d_{right}$
$W_{left} * 4 \text{ units} = 40N * 2 \text{ units}$
$W_{left} = (40N * 2 \text{ units}) / (4 \text{ units}) = 20N$

The total weight supported by the bar is 40N + 10N = 60N.

This value also corresponds to the reading of the dynamo-meter.

13. D

The bar weight tries to rotate the system clockwise. The weight is exerted at middle of the bar (d_w = 3 units). This is balanced by the pulling force of the rope exerted at 4 units away from the turning point (support). Thus, the upward force exerted by the rope is calculated by

$W_{bar} d_w = F_{rope} * d_F$

From the figure, you can see that the rope is connected to a combined pulley system (one fixed and one movable). Thus, given that only the movable pulley provides a gain in force (precisely double), we have for F_{rope} = 2 * 3N = 6N. So, we can write

$W_{bar} * 3 \text{ units} = 6N * 4 \text{ units}$
$W_{bar} = (6N * 4 \text{ units}) / (3 \text{ units}) = 8N$

14. B

The mechanical advantage of a lever (second class in the specific case) is calculated in two ways:

MA = W/F   or   MA = d_F/dW

The second equation is more suitable here, as we have enough information. So,

MA = 1m/20cm = 1m/0.2m = 5

15. C

The effort is represented here through the letter F (force). Thus, given that in pivoting systems in equilibrium

$W \cdot d_w = F \cdot d_F$

The equation becomes, after the substitutions,

400 N · 20cm = 100N · d_F
d_F = (400 N · 20cm) / 100N
= 80cm

16. D

The door handle has a turning effect when a force acts on it. Therefore, it is an example of a Lever (first class) as the turning point is between the force and load (they are on opposite sides of the door).

17. D

To create equilibrium, we must have:

$P \cdot d_P = F \cdot d_F$

If the required force distance d_F is denoted by x, the load distance d_P is 120 – x. Thus, we can write

100 · (120 - x) = 20 · x

Simplifying both sides by 20, the equation becomes,

5 · (120 - x) = x

5 · 120 – 5 · x = x

5 · 120 = x + 5x

600 = 6x

X = 600/6 = 100cm

Spatial Visualization

1. D
2. C
3. D
4. C
5. A
6. B
7. A
8. D
9. D
10. C

11. B
If two pieces have the same number at the position shown, it means that point is a junction point. Here, the hoses are at the central holes of the lateral faces of the platform, the screw-like shape is on top of the platform and the small cuboids act as legs.

12. B
If two pieces have the same number at the position shown, it means that point is a junction point. Following this rule, here will find that the correct assembly is shown at A.

13. D
If two pieces have the same number at the position shown, it means that point is a junction point. Here, the long rod is half above and half below the rectangular platform; the disc is at bottom of the rod, and the small rectangular shapes are in a vertical position at the extremities of the big rectangular platform, where the first is below the platform (the one on the right) and the other is above it (the one on the left).

14. B
Block A touches 6 blocks (1 is below, 2 are lateral in vertical position (narrow face), 2 are lateral in the horizontal position and one is lateral in the vertical position (wider side).

15. A
Block B touches 1 block below, 2 blocks above and one block laterally, i.e. in total 4 blocks.

16. B
Block C touches 3 blocks in total: all of them above it.

17. C
Since there are 5 cubes in the longest row, we need $5 \times 5 \times 5 = 125$ cubes in total to form a perfect cube.

First, let's count the existing cubes. In the first row, there are $5 + 4 + 5 + 5 + 4 = 23$ cubes.

In the second row, there are $5 + 3 + 4 + 4 + 1 = 17$ cubes.
In the third row, there are $3 + 3 + 2 = 8$ cubes.
In the fourth row, there are $3 + 3 + 1 = 7$ cubes.

Thus, in total there are $23 + 17 + 8 + 7 = 55$ cubes.

Hence, we must add $125 - 55 = 70$ cubes to form a perfect big cube.

18. A
There are 4 kinds of shapes that are on the lateral sides of the vertical bar. These shapes vary in length. You may notice that on the right side, the second shortest shape is missing. Thus, it must be placed in that part to balance the system.

19. A
The existing figure has 4 rows and 5 columns, where not all of them are complete. To be a perfect square, it must have 5 × 5 dimensions.

From the figure, the first row is complete. In the second row one cube is missing, in the third row two cubes are missing, in the fourth row four cubes are missing and in the fifth row all 5 cubes are missing. There missing cubes must be filled with one of the shapes.

The only shape that fits the description is the first one.

20. B
A large perfect cube is formed when it has the dimensions 4 × 4 × 4.

The first row is complete, the second row has one cube missing, the third row has another cube is missing, and the fourth, upper row, 1 + 3 + 0 + 1 = 5 cubes are missing.

Hence, in total, 1 + 1 + 5 = 7 cubes are missing to form a perfect cube.

The 3-Step Search Speed-Reading for Technical Manuals

Mastering Indexes, Tables of Contents, and Scanning for Keywords

The Trap: Most candidates treat the Code Book or Technical Manual like a novel. They start at the beginning of a paragraph and read until the end.

The Reality: On the STAR test, you don't have time to read. You have time to hunt.

The Skilled Trades readiness test is often an "open book" or "reference-available" exam. This is not a gift; it is a test of your speed. Your goal is not to understand the entire chapter; it is to find one specific number in less than 90 seconds.

You must stop "reading" and start "locating."

The Strategy: The 3-Step Search

Do not dive into the book until you know exactly what you are looking for. Follow this strict protocol.

Step 1: Extract the "DNA" (Keywords)

Ignore the fluff. A test question is 80% useless grammar and 20% critical data. You need to strip the sentence down to its "DNA"—the unique keywords.

Question: "According to the manufacturer's specifications, what is the maximum torque setting for a Grade 5, 1/2-inch bolt?"

The Fluff: "According to," "specifications," "what is the," "setting for a."

The DNA (Keywords): Torque, Grade 5, 1/2-inch.

Rule: Never search for common words like "bolt" or "setting." Search for the unique identifiers.

Step 2: Choose Your Map (Index vs. Table of Contents)

Once you have your keywords, you have two ways to enter the book. Choosing the wrong one will cost you 2 minutes.

Use the TABLE OF CONTENTS (TOC) When...

- Example: The question is about "Ladders."
- You need to browse a whole section.
- Speed Rating: Slow & Broad
- Speed Rating: Slow & Broad

Use the INDEX When...

- Example: The question is about "Flash Point."
- You need a specific page number immediately.
- Speed Rating: Fast & Precise
- Speed Rating: Fast & Precise

The "Back of the Book" Rule:

Always check the Index (back of the book) first. It is alphabetically organized and usually gives you the exact page or paragraph number. Only use the Table of Contents if the Index comes up empty.

Step 3: The Spiral Scan (Don't Read Left-to-Right)

Once you are on the right page, stop reading. If you read left-to-right, you are moving too slow.

The Technique:
1.   Use your finger. It forces your eye to focus.
2.   Scan for the "Shape" of the answer.

If the answer is a measurement, scan for numbers 10m, 50ft.

If the answer is a rule, scan for Bold Text or headings.

If the answer is a chemical property, look for the Table.

Visual Training: How to Scan Data Tables

In the trades, answers are rarely in sentences. They are in charts, load tables, and span tables. You need to master the "Cross-Hairs" method.

The Challenge:
"What is the maximum span for a 2x8 floor joist with a snow load of 40psf and spacing of 16 inches O.C.?"

How to Scan It (The Cross-Hairs Method):

Don't read the whole table.

1. Vertical Scan (Top to Bottom): Find the "Joist Size" column on the far left. Put your left finger on 2x8.

2. Horizontal Scan (Left to Right): Find the "Spacing" row or column headers. Find 16".

3. The Crash: Move your left finger across and your right finger down until they crash. The number where they meet is your answer.

Tip: If the question involves "Snow Load," ensure you are in the correct section of the table before you start scanning.

Visual Training: The WHMIS Sheet (SDS) Scan

Safety Data Sheets (SDS) are standardized. You don't need to read them; you need to know the "Geography" of the page.

The 3 Zones of an SDS:

If a question asks about...

1. "Danger" or "First Aid": Jump immediately to Section 2 (Hazards) or Section 4 (First Aid). Do not look at the bottom of the page.
2. "Flash Point" or "Smell/Appearance": Jump to Section 9 (Physical Properties). This is where the numbers are.
3. "PPE" or "Ventilation": Jump to Section 8 (Exposure Controls).

Drill:

Open a WHMIS sheet.

Find "Flash Point." (Goal: < 5 seconds)

Find "Skin Contact First Aid." (Goal: < 5 seconds)

Find "CAS Number." (Goal: < 3 seconds)

If you are reading the paragraphs, you are losing.

Summary Checklist: The Speed Reader's Mindset

[ ] I do not read sentences; I hunt for keywords.

[ ] I check the Index first, not the Table of Contents.

[ ] I use my finger to guide my eyes.

[ ] When looking for a number, I ignore all words and scan only for digits.

[ ] I know the "Geography" of a WHMIS sheet and standard Code Tables.

Digital Trades Data Entry, Graphs, and Tablet Testing

Navigating Digital Forms and Interpreting Computerized Charts

The Reality Check: The days of dirty clipboards are ending. On modern job sites, you clock in on an iPad, you read blueprints on a tablet, and you submit safety reports via a smartphone app.

Consequently, the Skilled Trades Assessment Readiness (STAR) test and many provincial exams have evolved. They now test "Digital Literacy." You don't need to be a computer programmer, but you must prove you can extract information from a screen and enter data correctly.

This chapter teaches you how to "read" a screen.

Part 1: The Spreadsheet Scan (The "Grid" Logic)
A spreadsheet is just a fancy tape measure: it has a horizontal axis (Rows) and a vertical axis (Columns). On the test, you will be shown a "Daily Log" or "Inventory List" and asked to find a specific detail.

The Trap: Candidates fail because they skim visually instead of using the "Grid Coordinates."

The Rule:

Identify the Column Header (Top).

Identify the Row Label (Left).

Find the intersection (The Cell).

PRACTICE DRILL: The Digital Daily Log
Review the sample "Digital Site Log" below and answer the questions.

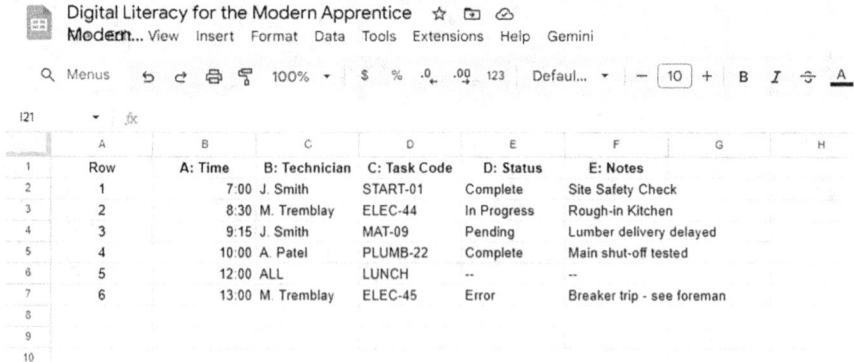

Question 1: Refer to the Digital Site Log. What is the status of the task performed by A. Patel?

How to solve:
Scan Column B for "A. Patel". (Found in Row 4).
Move across Row 4 to Column D (Status).

Answer: Complete.

Question 2 (The "inference" question):

Refer to the Digital Site Log. Which task code resulted in a safety error requiring the foreman?

How to solve:

1. Scan Column E (Notes) for the keyword "Foreman." (Found in Row 6).
2. Move backwards across Row 6 to Column C (Task Code).

Answer: ELEC-45.

Part 2: Graph Literacy (Trends vs. Numbers)

Digital tests often show you a graph generated by a machine (like a pressure monitor or thermostat). You need to interpret the Trend.

The 3 Directions
Don't just look at the numbers; look at the slope of the line.

1. Rising Line (/): The variable is increasing. (e.g., Temperature is getting hotter).
2. Falling Line (\ ): The variable is decreasing. (e.g., Pressure

is dropping).

3. Flat Line (—): The variable is Stable or Constant.

PRACTICE DRILL: Reading the Chart

Imagine a line graph showing "Hydraulic Pressure (PSI)" over "Time (Hours)."

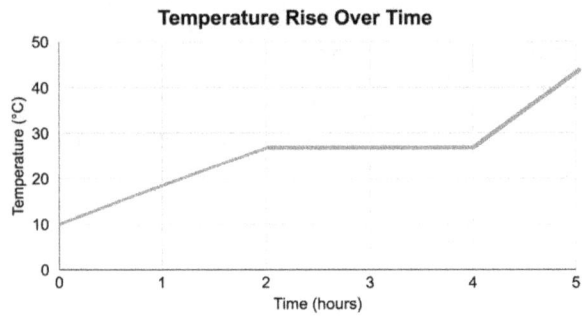

0-2 Hours: The line goes up steeply.
2-4 Hours: The line is perfectly flat.
4-5 Hours: The line drops straight down.

Question: Between hour 2 and hour 4, what is happening to the system?

    a. The system is overheating.
    b. The pressure is increasing rapidly.
    c. The pressure is stable/constant.
    d. The system has shut down.

The Answer is C.

Why? A flat line means the vertical value (Pressure) did not change. It doesn't mean the machine is off; it means it is holding steady.

Part 3: Data Entry & "Drop-Down" Discipline

In the "Skills for Success" framework, accuracy is more important than speed. A typo in a digital logbook can cause a billing error or a safety violation.

Common Test Interfaces:

Radio Buttons (Circles): You can only choose ONE option (Yes OR No).

Checkboxes (Squares): You can choose MULTIPLE options (Safety Boots AND Glasses).

Drop-Down Menus: You must select from a pre-set list.

The "Syntax" Trap

Computers are stupid. They need exact matches.

Dates: If the form asks for DD/MM/YYYY, entering May 5th, 2025 is WRONG.

  Correct: 05/05/2025

Units: If the box says "Weight (kg)", entering 50kg might be marked wrong because you added the letters "kg".

  Correct: 50 (Just the number).

PRACTICE DRILL: Spot the Error

The Task: Complete the incident report form using the data provided.

Date: November 12, 2024
ID: 445-A
Cost: $500.00

Candidate Entry:
Date: 11-12-24
Employee ID: 445 a
Est Cost: $500

Why this fails:

1. Date: The computer might read "24" as the year 0024. Always use the full year (2024) unless told otherwise.

2. ID: "445 a" has a space and a lowercase letter. The ID is "445-A". Case sensitivity matters.

3. Cost: The system often adds the "$" symbol automatically. Typing it twice ($$500) causes an error.

Part 4: Tablet Navigation (The "Hidden" Menus)

On a tablet-based test, you might not see all the information at once.

1. The "Hamburger" Menu

Look for three horizontal lines in the corner. This is the universal symbol for "Menu." If you can't find a page, tap the burger.

2. The Scroll Bar

Warning: Just because you see the "Next" button doesn't mean you are done. Always scroll to the very bottom of the window. Test makers love to hide a final "Signature" or "Confirmation" box below the visible screen area.

3. Zooming

On blueprint questions, you must "Pinch to Zoom." Do not guess at a measurement from the zoomed-out view. Zoom in until the pixelation is clear to get the exact number.

Summary Checklist: Digital Readiness

[ ] **Grid Logic:** I can find information by cross-referencing Row and Column.

[ ] **Trend Spotting:** I can tell if a graph shows a stable, rising, or falling value.

[ ] **Format Discipline:** I check the required date format (DD/MM vs MM/DD) before typing.

[ ] **Case Sensitivity:** I type codes exactly as they appear (Capital letters and hyphens included).

[ ] **The Scroll:** I always scroll to the bottom of a digital page before clicking "Submit."

Diagnostics & Troubleshooting

What to do after you take a practice test

Go through your answers carefully. For each wrong answer, refer to the explanation, and work through the questions step-by-step.

What kind of question (e.g. science, algebra, basic math etc.)

Look for patterns in your incorrect answers – what is it exactly that you are doing wrong or don't understand.
What types of questions do you have the most difficulty with? Refer to the tutorials and try to understand the questions.

Getting the Most from Practice Questions

Taking a practice test is probably the best way to prepare for a test.

Quick tips to get the most from practice questions:

Simulate Test Conditions

- Choose a quiet, distraction-free environment.

- Use a timer and allow just under 1 minute per question.

- Avoid using notes or online texts

Take it seriously -

- Treat the practice test as if it's the real exam -

- Familiarize yourself with the format and topics - this will reduce anxiety.

After Completing a Practice Test

Reviewing your work after you take a practice test is critical.

Immediate Review

- Make a note of any questions you found challenging or topics that felt unfamiliar or difficult.

- How was your time management?

- Overall comfort during the test?

Do a Thorough Review

- Go over your answers focusing on correct and incorrect answers.

- For incorrect answers, identify misunderstandings knowledge gaps or problem subject areas - here is where you need to spend your study time.

Look for Patterns

- Look for recurring themes in your errors to pinpoint specific areas needing improvement.

- Assess whether mistakes were due to content gaps, misinterpretation of questions, or time constraints.

JOB COMPLETE

Congratulations! You have made it to the end. By finishing this guide, you have shown the discipline and dedication required for a successful career in the skilled trades.

Passing this test is the first step toward securing your apprenticeship and building a rewarding future. You have put in the work—now trust your preparation.

Study. Practice. Succeed. We are rooting for you!

Don't Stop Now – Get Free Extras We want to make sure you are fully prepared. Register your copy to access free updates, additional test tips, and bonus practice questions.

Claim your extras here:

https://www.test-preparation.ca/register/

Digital Toolbox

How to Prepare for a Test - The Ultimate Guide

https://www.test-preparation.ca/prepare-test/

Learning Styles - The Complete Guide

https://www.test-preparation.ca/learning-style/

Test Anxiety Secrets!

https://www.test-preparation.ca/test-anxiety/

Time Management on a Test

https://www.test-preparation.ca/time-management/

Flash Cards - The Complete Guide

https://www.test-preparation.ca/flash-cards/

Test Preparation Video Series

https://www.test-preparation.ca/test-video/

How to Memorize - The Complete Guide

https://www.test-preparation.ca/memorize/

www.ingramcontent.com/pod-product-compliance
Lightning Source LLC
Chambersburg PA
CBHW071956070526
44583CB00015B/1209